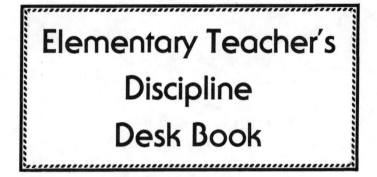

Elementary Teacher's Discipline Desk Book

Richard D. Shepardson

Parker Publishing Company, Inc.

West Nyack, New York

©1980, by

PARKER PUBLISHING COMPANY, INC.

West Nyack, New York

Library of Congress Cataloging in Publication Data

Shepardson, Richard.
 Elementary teacher's discipline desk book.

 Bibliography: p.
 Includes index.
 1. School discipline—Handbooks, manuals, etc.
2. Problem children—Education—Handbooks, manuals,
etc. I. Title.
LB3012.S53   372.15   80-16907
ISBN 0-13-260653-4

Printed in the United States of America

To Sheryl, Bruce, Carson and the
many other students who have had a profound
effect in shaping my teaching philosophy.

Introduction:
How to Benefit from
the Practical Ideas in This Desk Book

Discipline problems come in a seemingly unending array of sizes, shapes, and forms. All of us have our own horror stories and frustrations—the teasing, tattling, stealing, fighting, cursing, and other assorted headaches. Sometimes the problems are rather frustrating, sometimes they are pathetic, and sometimes they can be almost comical. However, the problems all force us to make decisions:

- What do you do when a six-year-old tells you to "sit on it and rotate"?
- What about the kid who lacks respect and his parents could care less?
- What do you do when Billy calls you an "S.O.B." and tells you he doesn't have to clear his desk?
- What about the pencil drop, the orange thrown against the blackboard, the shoe playfully tossed out the window?

We probably all wouldn't agree on the best answer to these problems but we can recognize some good alternatives. Answers do exist. Solutions have been found. Teachers have developed activities that capture student interest, techniques that channel enthusiasm, and strategies that effectively change behavior. Ideas that have been developed need to be shared; this is the moving force behind this book.

Classroom management is a complex issue. Given a problem situation, it's next to impossible to get a group of educators to agree on the "best" way to handle it. People have different goals, different values, and different perspectives. For any given problem, there are many situational factors—both past and present. This complexity, coupled with the lack of agreement among "experts" in the field, creates a natural breeding ground for disagreement, confusion, and frustration. Nevertheless, enough is known today about children, learning, and the behavior of organized groups to make classroom management highly predictable. We can discriminate between teachers who make efficient use of time and those who create dead time. We can discriminate between those who facilitate and those who block learning. We can discriminate between those who nurture and those who destroy class unity. *There is sufficient research, consistent with theory and practice, to enable us to identify and select effective activities, techniques, and strategies for managing children.*

Much of the material in this text results from teacher swaps and idea exchanges. Initially, principals were asked to identify teachers whom they felt were excellent in terms of classroom management. These teachers were then invited to submit two or three of their best ideas for managing a class. Many of the ideas in this text resulted from this exchange.

Basic to this text is the belief that the more ideas you have, the more effective you'll be as a teacher.

PRINCIPLE: **The more alternatives you have, the more effective you'll be.**

To illustrate, consider the small problem of a class becoming too noisy during an activity period. Rather than try to get the students' attention and tell them to quiet down, one of the following nonverbal signals could be used.

A Nonverbal Signal to Quiet the Room

During the work period, periodically draw arrows to let your class know how well they're working. The class knows that if the arrow touches the stop line, the activity is over—over in the sense that they have to put away their materials, clear their desks, and get ready for a quiet and highly structured session of worksheets and review work. (See Figure 1.)

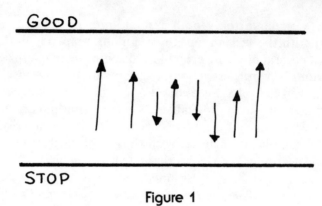

Figure 1

Traffic Control Center

When the classroom gets too noisy, go to the blackboard and draw part of a stop sign. The students know that when the sign is completed, the activity is over. (See Figure 2.)

Figure 2

A nonverbal signal like the two above gives you another tool and in many cases is more effective than a verbal reminder because you can get the message across without having to stop everything to get the class's attention. You can communicate your concerns without hollering and coming across as the "Old Ogre." In the above cases, as soon as you pick up the chalk, one or two students will take notice and they'll pass the word to quiet down. The end result will be peer pressure working for you, rather than against you. Teachers have successfully used these techniques at various grade levels and with a variety of activities. They do work.

What happens if you are troubled by something a little more serious? Let's say a couple of your shining lights are caught sticking straw wrappers, dipped in apple cobbler, to the cafeteria ceiling.

How do you react to such mischief? The following idea has worked in similar cases.

The Second Chance Letter

Take the children aside and tell them to write a letter to their parents telling exactly what they have done. When the letters are completed to your satisfaction, tell the students that you will not send the letters as long as they clean up the mess and don't pull a similar stunt. Impress upon the children that you don't expect them to do it again and certainly hope you don't have to send the letter to their parents.

A principal who tried this technique on several different occasions noted that it not only put an end to misbehavior, but it also helped build a sense of trust with the children involved.

Many of the ideas presented in this handbook will provide you with a fresh approach. The techniques represent a multifaceted and humanistic approach to developing responsible behavior. The emphasis is on capturing rather than coercing, engineering rather than reacting, building dignity rather than being punitive.

Listed below are some of the key principles developed in the text:

- Avoid public "win/lose" confrontations.
- Probe rather than pass premature judgment.
- Give students time to correct their errors.
- Concentrate on causes rather than on the misbehavior itself.
- Don't embarrass students or make them lose face in front of their classmates.
- Make frequent use of student ideas.
- Create numerous activities for students to allow them to contribute and feel important.
- In order to change behavior, you need to change perceptions.

These and other principles in the text are supported with specific ideas, techniques, and strategies that have been shared by teachers across the nation. The ideas are shared in the spirit and belief that *the more alternatives you have, the more effective you'll be.*

Richard D. Shepardson

Acknowledgments

The items presented in this book came from a variety of sources. Many were contributed by teachers in a series of idea exchanges. In these cases, the contributor's name, city, and state have been listed below the description of his or her idea. Some of these contributions are original, others represent adaptations of old standbys. I have tried to track down original sources, but this has been impossible to do in some cases. Contributors often cannot remember whether they picked up an idea from another teacher, a workshop, or some other forgotten source.

Besides the many teachers who have contributed, I would like to acknowledge the many top-notch professionals who have contributed indirectly, particularly the staffs of the Campbell Elementary School District (Campbell, California), Union Elementary School District (San Jose, California), and the Iowa City Community School District (Iowa City, Iowa). I have been especially influenced by a number of educators, many of whom I have never thanked directly. I am especially indebted to Mrs. Lincoln (Almaden Elementary), Mr. Solice (a student teacher at Almaden Elementary), Mrs. Mary Akita (Carlton Elementary), Mr. Earl Downing (Carlton Elementary), Mr. Casey Bernard (Carlton Elementary), Dr. Ramonda (San Jose State), and Dr. C. Ray Williams (University of Texas).

The cartoons and detailed sketches were done by Margie V. Gardner. Several drawings were contributed by Kathleen Lyons, and the photographic work was done by Cal Mether. Special thanks are extended to Dorian Bright-Walker for her secretarial support in preparing the manuscript.

I credit the completion of this book to my wife's support, encouragement, and patience. I am also deeply indebted to the rest of my family for their many sacrifices.

R.D.S.

Contents

1

Signals and Procedures
That Avoid Dead Time
and Eliminate Hassles

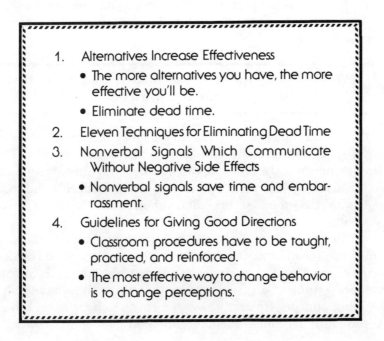

1. Alternatives Increase Effectiveness
   - The more alternatives you have, the more effective you'll be.
   - Eliminate dead time.
2. Eleven Techniques for Eliminating Dead Time
3. Nonverbal Signals Which Communicate Without Negative Side Effects
   - Nonverbal signals save time and embarrassment.
4. Guidelines for Giving Good Directions
   - Classroom procedures have to be taught, practiced, and reinforced.
   - The most effective way to change behavior is to change perceptions.

ALTERNATIVES INCREASE EFFECTIVENESS

The ideas presented in this chapter provide alternative ways of getting your students' attention, controlling movement, and directing students. The material is presented on the premise that choices increase effectiveness. The skilled professional can gracefully handle the unexpected, the different, the extreme. To do this, you need alternative strategies, different techniques, and a whole host of activities. As Figure 1-1 illustrates, there is power in alternatives.

PRINCIPLE: **The more alternatives you have, the more effective you'll be.**

This text translates theory into practice by taking a principle of classroom management and generating a host of ideas that demonstrate how the principle can be adapted or directly applied in your classroom. The ideas are selected on the basis of sound theory and with the hope of providing choices for handling diverse conditions.

This first chapter deals with a major contributor to classroom problems—dead time. Dead time is unproductive time and comes in many forms: the bored student sitting at his desk with his hand propped up in the air, unnecessary directions given habitually to knowing students, frustrating assignments which are either too easy or too hard, and idle students standing in line.

PRINCIPLE: **Eliminate dead time.**

Effective use of class time is directly related to teaching success. It's obvious that the more time you spend teaching, the greater the chance that your students will learn. The poor use of class time

Figure 1-1

has been one of the reasons why individualized programs have not produced desired results in terms of achievement. In many individualized programs, teachers spend too much time coordinating and taking care of clerical responsibilities and too little time teaching.

ELEVEN TECHNIQUES FOR ELIMINATING DEAD TIME

ITEM 1. Home Base

When you take your class into an open area, such as the gym, stage, or playground, establish a home base (see Figure 1-2). Have

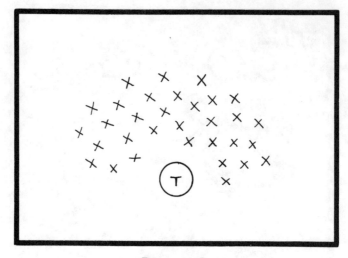

Figure 1-2

the students gather around you in a loose horseshoe arrangement. The place where the students squat or sit is their home base. Help them remember where they are sitting so they can return to exactly the same spot when the signal is given. Practice by having the students mill around for a few seconds, and then signal "home base." The students should immediately return to their spots. A whistle, a beat of a drum, a gavel, a bell, or some other sound can be used as the device to signal home base.

This technique saves time by eliminating the need to tell the class to assemble or line up. If they know what is expected, they respond quickly without unnecessary directions. Also, it eliminates the confusion caused by students fighting over a certain position in line.

ITEM 2. Use Visual Reference Points

Having students line up on a line is always easier than having them just line up somewhere. In the same vein, a set of 12-inch square vinyl or asbestos tiles can be used as handy reference points (see Figure 1-3). Numbers can be easily added with permanent Magic Markers. These can be used on the chalkboard, on ledges, on the floor, or on the walls.

These tiles can be used in a number of ways:

1. To designate areas where groups will meet.
2. To identify parts in a singing round.

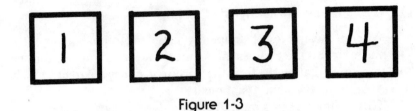

Figure 1-3

3. To designate an area of the chalkboard in which an individual or team will work a problem.

4. Outside, for relays or any other activity where you want groups to line up at a certain spot.

5. To designate team areas for classroom games.

6. In values clarification activities: "Line up on Number 1 if you agree with Response 1."

7. To sequence individual pictures or sentences from a story (or anything that can be ordered).

Glenna Tevis
Solon, Iowa

ITEM 3. A Reference Mark on the Student's Desk

In the first grade, a green dot placed on the left-hand side of a student's desk (name tag) and a red dot on the right-hand side make handy reference points. These can be used in giving left/right directions: "Start your name and all papers in the left-hand corner— green dot." They can be used when you want the students to put aside a tool or some other material: "While I read this part, put your clay on the red dot."

Patricia Watson
Algona, Iowa

ITEM 4. Assigned Partners

Assigning permanent partners saves time. With permanent partners, students know with whom to pair off ahead of time. It is a good idea to assign several permanent "rovers" to handle absentees. The partner arrangement can be used for simple drill activities, small discussion groups, sharing of materials, and field trips.

The procedure for pairing should be practiced each time new partners are assigned. Also, make sure that the new "rovers" know what they should do if someone is absent.

ITEM 5. Playing Music Signals Cleanup

When it is time for cleanup, ask a student to put on a record. The music signals the class that it is time to start cleaning up, and the students know that by the time the music ends, they are to be in their seats, ready for the next assignment.

This technique saves on the time involved in getting your class's attention and provides a pleasant reminder that they don't have all day to get ready for the next assignment.

ITEM 6. Catchy Phrases

Occasionally, when you get ready to give a direction, you can use a catchy phrase to get the students' attention:

- "Raise your hand if you're listening."
- "Will all the people talking please stand."
- "If you have purple hair, you may talk."

Mrs. Helen Rodgers
Crawfordsville, Iowa

Mrs. Betty Shadle
Clinton, Iowa

Comments: Humor adds variety and spice to what can become dull and routine. In the above case, the message is still there—"shape up"—yet the teacher is not coming across as an old ogre. It should be stressed that this technique should only be used once in a great while.

*Many of the problems which seem to gnaw away at teacher and class morale are part of institutional life. And, let's face it, school is an institution divided into organized groups. There has to be time spent waiting. During these times, children will act and react with the enthusiasm and energy characteristic of their age. **Don't treat each little disturbance as a serious act of defiance.** Use humor to get the message across in a pleasant manner.*

ITEM 7. Posting an Odd Time

When you ask students to be cleaned up by a certain time or ready to start at a certain time, use an odd time, such as 9:53. Students tend to comply and make a game out of being ready on time, whereas if you tell them to be ready at 10:00, they seem to be a little more lackadaisical in their approach. This technique is another one that can be easily overdone, so use it sparingly.

ITEM 8. Counting Down

You can use the technique employed by drive-in theaters to announce the beginning of the next attraction. Students respond better to a change in schedule if they have some advance notice. In the example of Figure 1-4, the teacher has gone to the board three times and will probably post two or three more warnings as needed.

Figure 1-4

ITEM 9. Class List

At the beginning of the year, ditto a list of the names of students in the class. Such lists are handy to use when children bring money for book clubs, school plays, etc. The room mothers use one and each child could be given one before Valentine's Day.

Mrs. Marcene Straub
Limon, Colorado

ITEM 10. Who Is Next?

The list of students (see Item 9) serves as an easy way to record who has had a turn painting at the art easel or putting up the calendar. Use a class list with a circle in front of each child's name. As each child takes his turn, he checks the circle, and it is easy to tell who is next.

Mrs. Ruth Nieman
Denver, Iowa

ITEM 11. Handling Homework Assignments for Absentees

In classes where many individual or small group assignments are given, use a "buddy system." Each student has a partner. It is the partner's responsibility to record missed assignments for the absent student. At the end of the day, these are checked with the teacher to see which assignments will in fact have to be made up. The student may then drop the list off along with the necessary books at the student's home, or other appropriate action may be taken (assignments may be telephoned to partner, or assignments and books may be taken to the office by the partner for a parent to pick up).

Mrs. Marcene Straub
Limon, Colorado

ITEM 12. Who Does What?

It seems to take so much time to ask each child what activity he would like to participate in during a free choice period. To eliminate some of the time consumed, make a chart listing and illustrating all activities for the period (see Figure 1-5). Each child is given a spring-type clothespin with his name on it. As it is given to the child, he places it on the chart beside (above or below) the activity of his choice. When the number of clothespins have been placed on any one activity as designated by the numbered squares, the child realizes that the activity is filled and that he must choose something else. This allows the child to determine when an activity has enough participants and when he has to make another choice.

Be sure to make provisions for at least five more children than you have enrolled in order that each child may have a choice and not have to take what is left over by the time it is his turn to make a choice.

Mrs. Flora D. Matthews
Miami, Florida

Comments: This idea can be adapted to make the system more flexible. Figure 1-6 shows how the checkout of interest centers can be organized with a pocket chart and individual clothespins. The child keeps his clothespins at his desk (or they can be filed in a central location). When he wants to work in a certain area, he just attaches his

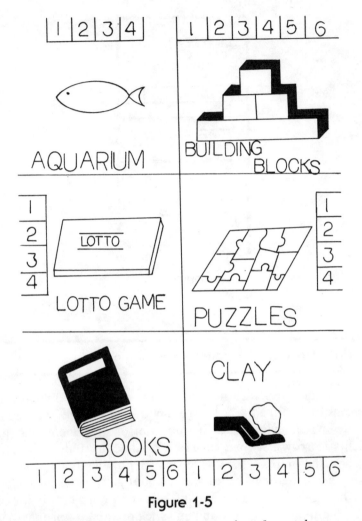

Figure 1-5

clothespin to the board. The number for each center indicates how many students are allowed to work in that area at one time. Children move eachother's clothespins.

ITEM 13. Plastic Buckets

A set of plastic tubs or plastic buckets can be used for dispersal as well as for cleanup. If you use several "cleanup stations" (buckets with paper towels), instead of expecting everyone to use the sink or restroom, you can eliminate potential problems and keep the janitor happy.

Figure 1-6

PRINCIPLE: **Use many dispersal points.**

Using one dispersal point is a common cause of management problems. As students converge on the one dispersal point, a shoving match may ensue. If you control movement and have students go a row at a time, there is "dead time" as students wait their turn. Furthermore, with one dispersal point, students who are waiting become upset as they worry about getting the culls. On the other hand, if you use multiple distribution points (a tray for each row), you minimize the waiting and the potential for problems and hard feelings.

ITEM 14. Cafeteria Trays

One year I was lucky enough to scrounge a set of cafeteria trays and a set of lockers from a remodeled junior high. The trays came in handy for getting materials ready to distribute. For example, prior to a lesson investigating the dissolving rate of Alka Seltzer, a student could set up trays for each group containing the needed graph paper, Alka Seltzer, spoons, and other material. In this way, the materials could be quickly distributed to each table without unnecessary commotion or "dead time."

ITEM 15. Plastic Bottles

Plastic jugs (1 gallon) can be cut out and used for storage of crayons, scissors, and similar materials (see Figure 1-7).

Mrs. Marilyn Kroll
Indianola, Iowa

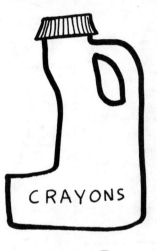

Figure 1-7

ITEM 16. Assignment Completed

This procedure serves as an easy way to keep a set of papers together and it also serves as a quick check to see who has completed an assignment.

As illustrated in Figure 1-8, the ditto is stapled to a worksheet and clipped to the outside of an envelope. The envelope can be pinned to the bulletin board or placed in some appropriate spot.

As the child finishes his work, he places it in the envelope and crosses off his name.

Janet Peters
Clinton, Iowa

ITEM 17. Use the Overhead Projector for Lettering Bulletin Boards

If you purchase an alphabet book, you can easily make labels for a display or bulletin board by tracing the letters onto a

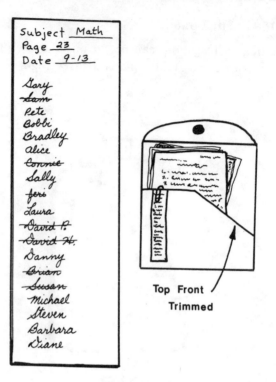

Subject __Math__
Page __23__
Date __9-13__

Gary
~~Sam~~
Pete
Bobbi
Bradley
alice
~~Connie~~
Sally
~~Jeri~~
Laura
~~David P.~~
~~David H.~~
Danny
~~Brian~~
~~Susan~~
Michael
Steven
Barbara
Diane

Top Front
Trimmed

Figure 1-8

transparency. The transparency can then be used with the overhead projector and, by varying the distance of the machine from your paper, you can easily trace any size letters you want.

Comments: The preceding ideas were selected because they have the potential for saving time. Use of time is important to successful classroom management in a number of ways: Dead time during which students sit idle breeds discipline problems, and it should be avoided. Quality use of time can help build a positive, stimulating atmosphere which captures student interest. Productive use of your limited time will help you develop a positive mental attitude and a relaxed learning atmosphere.

These ideas and many that follow are designed to give students responsibility, reduce the amount of time devoted to routine maintenance, and free the teacher for more important matters.

NONVERBAL SIGNALS WHICH COMMUNICATE
WITHOUT NEGATIVE SIDE EFFECTS

Nonverbal signals are less disruptive in the sense that you don't have to stop a class and get everyone's attention to give them a message. This avoids many of the hassles and conflicts that can occur as you try to trim the sails and take another tack.

PRINCIPLE: **Nonverbal signals save time and embarrassment.**

Another advantage of many nonverbal signals is that once they are given, you can direct your personal attention to deviates without holding the rest of the class at bay. Thus, if you have to give special reminders or clarification, you can do so privately without embarrassing the student or appearing ugly in front of the class.

ITEM 18. A Nonverbal Signal to Quiet the Room

As the class works, draw two lines on the board. As in Figure 1-9, the top line is labeled "Good" and the bottom is "Stop." During the work period, draw arrows to monitor your students' behavior. If an arrow touches the "Stop" line, the activity is over.

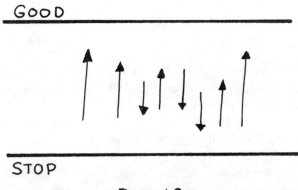

Figure 1-9

ITEM 19. Traffic Light

A simulated traffic light can be made so that it can rest on the chalk tray (see Figure 1-10). During an activity period when no

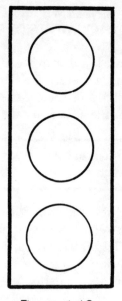

Figure 1-10

conversation is permitted, a red circle can be hung or taped onto the top light. If some conversation is permitted, remove the red circle and add the yellow. When considerable movement and conversation are permitted, put up the green. In this way, students know what is expected. (Note: The signal could be drawn on the chalkboard and colored circles taped as needed.)

Nancy Schroht
Owatonna, Minnesota

The same idea can be used to monitor student noise as well as indicate what is desirable. As in Figure 1-11, colored paper is used on all three lights and an arrow is added.

The arrow always starts at green. When someone (student or teacher) thinks it is beginning to get too noisy, he moves the arrow to yellow announcing that fact. If the noise returns to an acceptable level, the arrow is moved back to the green section. If the noise does not decrease, the arrow is moved to the red section. This brings the activity to a stop and time is taken to iron out the difficulty. Usually all that is needed to achieve the desired results is for the arrow to be moved to the yellow light.

Peg Dunlap
Cedar Rapids, Iowa

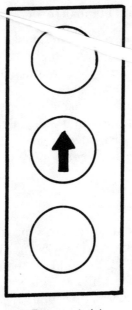

Figure 1-11

ITEM 20. Traffic Control Center

Designate a certain portion of the blackboard as the "Traffic Control Center." When the classroom gets too noisy, go to the area and draw part of a stop sign. As in Figure 1-12, you might draw one or two sides or some of the letters, depending on the situation and how long the activity will run. The students should know that if the stop sign is completed, the activity stops.

Mrs. Flora D. Matthews
Miami, Florida

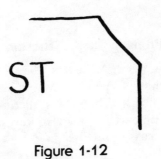

Figure 1-12

ITEM 21. Thumbs Up/Thumbs Down

Students can have a set of silent signals to indicate their general agreement or disagreement with a comment or problem worked on the board; thumbs up for agree, thumbs down for disagree, and finger on chin for confusion.

The same basic idea could be used during a testing period. If a student needs more time, he could indicate that by raising a closed fist. The teacher could easily discriminate the closed fist from the raised hand. The closed fist signals more time is needed; the hand signals a question.

ITEM 22. Listening Cue

Explain your reasons to the class for why it is important that you know when they are ready to listen, and then have the class suggest possible cues that they could use to show that they're paying attention. For example, while working with a small group of primary students, a teacher might put her finger on her nose and wait until all children in her group did the same before giving directions.

Mrs. Lynn Simmons
Denver, Colorado

ITEM 23. Quiet Sign

Raising a forefinger in the air above the head can signal the need to lower room noise. This is done without any voice and can be used by teachers and students. Students can take the initiative when they sense that the room is getting too loud. When one student observes another student or the teacher giving the sign, he is expected to join in, giving the sign to his neighbors.

Mrs. Robert Arthaud
Oelwein, Iowa

ITEM 24. Using Props to Shape Behavior

A variety of nonverbal cues can be used to alert students to desired types of behavior. You can have a certain spot in the room for discussing problems. When the students see you sitting there, they know a problem exists. They also know that they're supposed to join you and discuss the problem.

Another technique is to use a certain chair to signal the fact that you are going to assume a particular response behavior. A stool could be used every time you plan to assume a nonjudgmental, accepting strategy. This can be done without any direct mention of the fact. Consistently use it and it will gradually shape the students' behavior.

Picking up a pointer could be used to signal a drill session. When the teacher picks up the pointer and flashes on the overhead, the students know they're to get out a piece of paper and get ready for a formal drill session. They are ready for the first problem without any verbal direction from the teacher. Of course, all of these techniques have to be introduced and will occasionally need reinforcement and reminders.

ITEM 25. "Islands"—Student's Signal for Privacy

Carpet squares, cut into odd shapes, can be used as "islands." When a child wants to work or play alone, he takes an island and his materials to an open area. The island signals the other students that he will not bother anyone and no one should bother him. "Island chains" (several carpets joined together) can also be used.

Stephanie Y. Norton
Rock Island, Illinois

ITEM 26. Privacy Boards

As shown in Figure 1-13, the top, bottom, and one side of a cardboard box serve nicely as a three-sided carrel. These store easily and work well on a student's desk.

Stephanie Y. Norton
Rock Island, Illinois

Figure 1-13

ITEM 27. Signal Materials Needed

When beginning a project, instead of always saying what materials are needed, put up the appropriate pictures (see Figure 1-14). Students respond by getting out the necessary items.

Mrs. Karen Asa
Algona, Iowa

Figure 1-14

ITEM 28. Egg Timer Signals End of Activity

An egg timer is a helpful addition to the classroom. Set the timer for the amount of time the students need for such activities as assignments or reading. The responsibility is now placed on the bell, rather than the teacher, to tell everyone when it is time to put the activity away.

Susanne Bartz
Mason City, Iowa

> **Comments:** *Nonverbal signals save time and limit the number of times you have to ask for the class's attention. They communicate effectively and usually free the teacher to make individual contacts rather than force the teacher to stand stoically waiting for the group's attention.*

GUIDELINES FOR GIVING GOOD DIRECTIONS

Members of a class often have to start together, move together, and stop together. Because of this, a "task-oriented" or "businesslike" atmosphere is conducive to learning and should not be viewed as dehumanizing. You should establish procedures and routines to avoid unnecessary commotion and dead time.

- "We have seen how they gathered their food. Now, let's look at how they prepared it."
- "Our first step is ..."

4. Do not pass out materials until you have given all directions.

If you pass out materials and then call for the students' attention, you have a built-in problem.

ITEM 30. Magic Words

Use a "magic word" to avoid the problem of students starting before you have finished giving directions. "Don't start until you hear the magic word—*katzenjammer*. Today, *katzenjammer* is our magic word for starting projects."

Ginny Clark
Iowa City, Iowa

Comments: Clarity is an important dimension of effective teaching. You can be more explicit by: (1) cueing students on how to respond, (2) using visual reference points, (3) using structuring comments, and (4) getting students to rephrase the directions. In addition, when it comes to introducing a new signal or procedure, be sure to clearly explain the rationale for the new procedure and be clear in explaining exactly what behavior is and is not desired. Remember to give students a chance to practice any new procedure. Procedures have to be taught and reinforced just as any other skill or concept is taught and reinforced.

SUMMARY

Dead time is a major contributor to classroom control problems. Dead time is created when students sit idly waiting for the teacher to write something on the board. It is created when students wait for the teacher to help them. It is created when instructional time is used inappropriately. It is created when a teacher stops the whole class to give directions to a few or to tell the class that they're getting too noisy. It results when teachers play an overly dominant role which does not allow students to make decisions and act independently.

When students sit idly, they usually find something to do or some way to entertain themselves. This type of dead time will frequently result in minor discipline problems chipping away at morale. Dead time, in terms of inappropriate lessons, can add frustration which festers into more serious discipline problems. As teachers, we need to constantly be on the alert for ways to eliminate or cut down on dead time.

Signals and procedures help reduce unproductive time. They encourage a "task-oriented" or "businesslike" atmosphere, an atmosphere which is conducive to learning, one which should not be viewed as dehumanizing. Because classrooms are organized groups and have certain needs, a class needs to move together, work together, and stop together. Nonverbal signals can be given without the teacher having to get the attention of the whole class. The more dominant the teacher becomes in directing the group along those lines, the more dead time results. The more dead time, the more problems. *Building independence should be a major thrust of all teachers.*

2

Using Materials and Activities
to Stimulate Student Involvement

1. "Hands-On" Materials Capture Student Interest
   - Concrete experiences enhance learning at all levels.
   - Manipulating objects has motivational appeal in and of itself.
2. Place Students in an Active Role
   - Constraints increase student motivation.
   - Teacher vulnerability increases learning potential.

As stressed in Chapter 1, perceptions are the key to successful classroom management. If students perceive your class as a desirable place to be, they will cooperate. If they perceive your class as being desirable, they will want to belong and will be more willing to follow class norms. Therefore, it becomes important to consciously nourish and cultivate positive student perceptions.

You can build positive perceptions by placing students in an active role and providing direct "hands-on" experiences.

"HANDS-ON" MATERIALS HELP CAPTURE STUDENT INTEREST

Children need to touch and handle things; they need to experience the real world. As we handle an object, we begin to ask questions about it. An arrowhead in a display case is very different from an arrowhead in the palm. Just looking at it leaves learning at the sterile level. Holding an arrowhead, as in Figure 2-1, makes it come alive: "What was the person like who first fashioned this piece of work? How was it used? How sharp is the edge? How much pressure would be needed before I would cut my skin?"

Handling an object gives us a familiarity with it. This handling, or educational play, is an important aspect of learning. We don't learn about a vise grip by looking at a picture (see Figure 2-2) or reading a description of it. We begin to know this tool as we handle it and use it in a variety of situations. We begin to know it as we compare its work with that of other tools.

PRINCIPLE: **Concrete experiences enhance learning at all levels.**

To talk to a student or class about an object or process they have not experienced is a good example of "empty verbalism." We forget the incidental knowledge, the vast array of experiences, facts,

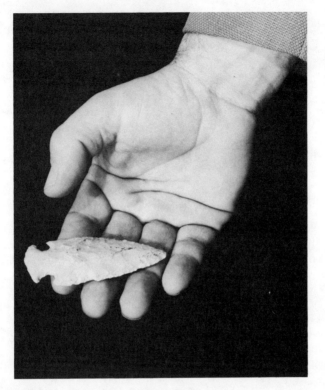

Figure 2-1

associations, and interrelationships we build up over the years. We assume too much. I remember giving what I thought was an excellent description of a card game (Oklahoma Rummy) to a new acquaintance. After I reviewed the game, my self-satisfaction was shattered when my guest innocently asked, "What's a face card?" Just because we have experienced something, just because we are familiar with the component parts, we shouldn't assume that everyone else is, too. Empty verbalism finds its way into the classroom all too frequently. We need to provide time for handling, manipulating, comparing, and just getting acquainted with new ideas and new materials.

PRINCIPLE: **Manipulating objects has motivational appeal in and of itself.**

One way to cut down management problems is to make your

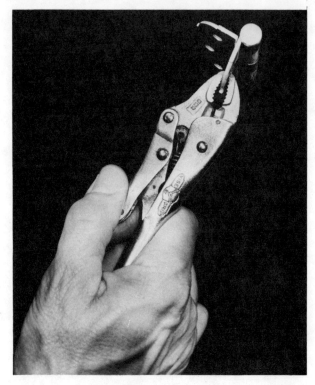

Figure 2-2

room more interesting. Bringing in objects for the students to handle can help accomplish this.

The city water meter pictured in Figure 2-3 was an object that really intrigued my students. By taking the machine apart and using a hacksaw, one of my fifth graders laboriously made a cross-sectional cut in the water meter. The students were fascinated by the gears and spent many free moments spinning the gears and watching the numbers in the meter change. The meter kept many idle hands busy. The physical activity, in and of itself, had great appeal.

ITEM 31. Collections

The use of concrete objects also forces you to go outside the school's walls and bring in some of the real world. An effective way to bring in the outside world is to feature weekly collections. Set up a table as a "Collection Display Area." Establish some device for dividing the table into two areas: (1) materials that can be handled, and (2) materials that are not to be handled. On the first of the

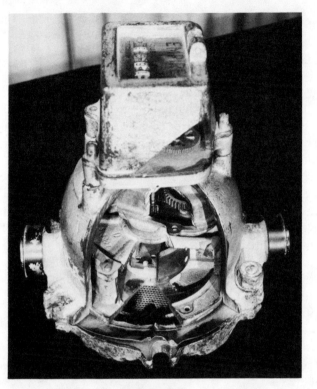

Figure 2-3

month, post the themes for the coming weeks. You might consider the following:

1. *Nails.* Challenge your class to see how many different kinds of nails they can bring in. Ask them to tape or glue their specimens to a piece of cardboard or heavy paper.

2. *Cylinders.* Bring in anything you want that is cylindrical in shape.

3. *Blue and round.* Bring in anything that is basically round in shape and has blue coloring somewhere on it.

4. *Measuring devices.*

5. *Exercising devices.* Three of my boys, ages 9-11, devised a system for qualifying as Super Heroes: If you could pull the rope through the Apollo Exerciser when it was set at 190, then you had the strength of 190 men. If you could run the 50-yard dash in less than 9 seconds you were a Mercury Flash; if you could do it in under 8 seconds, you were a

Double Mercury Flash. With this kernel idea, I'm sure a group could develop a whole array of tests and titles.

ITEM 32. Workshop

A workshop can be made using a piece of pegboard attached to a 1″ × 12″ shelving board (see Figure 2-4). Various tools and materials can be stored on the pegboard, such as hammer, small saw, screwdriver, nails, various decorative brads, pinking shears, white glue, colored tape, gum labels, stars, masking tape, scraps of wood, wire, string, and a junk box containing anything from acorns to zippers. Students, given the responsibility, can learn how to use and put away the tools and materials. This center can add a very enjoyable and creative dimension to your classroom. The flag sketched in Figure 2-5 is one idea that grew out of the availability of the tools and materials. Student-made flags were attached to the desks, raised every morning, and lowered at the end of class. Little things like this have an accumulative "big effect" on student perceptions.

Figure 2-4

ITEM 33. Following Directions

For this activity you will need the makings for a peanut butter and jelly sandwich, a plastic glove (you may also want an apron), a knife, napkins, and a plate.

Have your students write a composition on "How to Make a Peanut Butter and Jelly Sandwich." After they finish, pick a composition at random and try to make a sandwich doing specifically what the composition tells you to do. For example, if the

Figure 2-5

composition does not specifically state, "Remove the cover from the peanut butter jar," you will not be able to make the sandwich. If the writer does not specifically tell you to pick up a knife, you should dig into the jar with your gloved finger and use it to smear the peanut butter.

Pick two or three more compositions from the group and try again. The use of the real thing helps develop language skills and, more importantly, contributes to your students' general positive tone toward their work, their class, and you, their teacher.

Alberta Thien
Muscatine, Iowa

ITEM 34. Gingerbread Man (A Unit for Kindergarten)

To start the year off with a bang, devote one of your bulletin boards to the "Gingerbread Man." Read the story to your class and talk about the Gingerbread Man's adventures. On the next day, have students make the Gingerbread Man in class. Some of the children can beat the eggs, add the flour, and so on. Then, have the cook or a parent bake the Gingerbread Man. This is where the fun begins.

In advance, give the cook a brown paper gingerbread man, with a note saying, "Ha, come catch me. I ran away from the cook, and I can run away from you. I can! I can!" Add a clue to the note indicating where the class can find the Gingerbread Man: "Try and catch me, I'm in the office!" Following this clue, take the class to the office to find the Gingerbread Man. After the students have been introduced to the office, the secretary or principal might produce another note: "Ha! I ran away again. Look for a note on your teacher's desk tomorrow. Maybe you'll find me."

You can use a series of clues and run this activity for several days. The clues should lead the class to each of the important parts of the building.

It is also a good idea to send home a note (see Figure 2-6) keeping parents informed of the activity and providing a recipe for the Gingerbread Man.

Nancy Story
Montezuma, Iowa

ITEM 35. Estimating

As an interest center or as part of the math activity, students can estimate the following:

1. Number of peas in a jar.
2. Weight of a math book.
3. Drops in a thimble (use an eyedropper).
4. Breaths it takes to fill a balloon.
5. Words in a newspaper article.
6. Acres of land in the school yard.
7. Kernels of corn on an ear.

When all the estimates are in, you can have the class discuss ways to count the items in question. More accurate methods to estimate could be devised or actual counts could be made.

Kerry Aiken
Tama, Iowa

ITEM 36. Owl Pellets

This idea, although it may sound a little bizarre, has great motivational value for some students. I used it successfully in

Dear Mom and Dad,

We certainly had fun with our friend, the Gingerbread Boy. In case you'd like to make a Gingerbread Boy at home, here is the recipe.

⅔ cup shortening	1 tsp. cinnamon
1¼ cups sugar	½ tsp. nutmeg
2 Tbsp. molasses	2 Tbsp. sour milk
2 eggs	3 C. flour
1 tsp. soda	1 tsp. baking powder
1 tsp. salt	½ tsp. ginger

Cream shortening and sugar. Add eggs and molasses. Add sour milk in which soda has been dissolved. Add flour which has been sifted with salt, baking powder, and spices. Roll in a thin sheet. Cut with floured cutter. Place on a greased baking sheet. Bake in a 375 degree oven for about 7 minutes.

But, do you know what? When we went to get the Gingerbread Boy from the cooks, he had run away. We went to the Senior High Office to look for him. But we didn't find him. We will look for him again tomorrow. I sure hope we find him soon.

Love,

Figure 2-6

motivating a group of nine- and ten-year-old boys who were very reluctant readers, operating approximately three years below grade level.

An owl eats its food whole and cannot digest the fur, bones, seed coats, and parts of insect bodies which it eats. These are regurgitated somewhat like a cat regurgitates a hair ball. The owl pellets are usually 1 to 3 inches in length. They are odorless, because the owl's gastric juices have sterilized the material, and they are safe to handle.

Using tweezers and probes (see Figure 2-7), you can carefully pull the pellets apart and examine the contents to see what the owl has been eating. Once you find an owl's roost, you can usually go

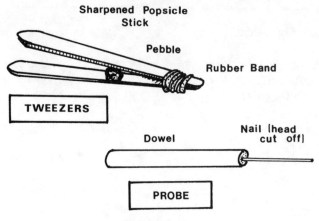

Figure 2-7

back to the same spot and gather more pellets. On a single visit, I have found as many as 80 pellets under a roost in a palm tree in a downtown cemetery in San Jose, California. If you find several roosts, you can compare the diets of the different birds.

Students can make interesting displays of their findings, they can write fictional stories about the owl's life, or they can make a chart displaying the food web using the remains found in the pellets. If you're interested in this idea, read "The Owl Pellet," by Gilbert C. Yee, *Science and Children,* May 1969, Vol. 6, No. 8, p. 9.

> **Comments:** *Concrete objects add variety, stimulate interest, and enhance learning. Classroom management is multifaceted, and you're not going to be successful if you look for simple solutions to behavior problems. Finding harsher punishments won't do the trick. More sophisticated behavior modification systems won't do it. You have to approach the problem from many angles. Your program should be one of the first places you look. The use of "hands-on" materials will make your lessons more enjoyable and more effective. Hands-on materials stimulate student questions, add realism, provide tactile stimulation, and add variety. They help capture rather than coerce students.*

ACTIVITIES WHICH PLACE STUDENTS IN AN ACTIVE ROLE

This section contains a variety of teaching strategies which stress student participation. Active student involvement leads to fewer discipline problems by increasing motivation. The following activities and strategies force students to ask questions, to generate hypotheses, to collect and interpret data, and to test hypotheses. The activity generated is not activity for activity's sake, but activity designed to encourage students to think and to trust their thinking. The students are forced into decision making. They're active; thus, motivation increases.

PRINCIPLE: **Constraints increase student motivation.**

Constraints have been used to motivate for many years. Most games employ some type of constraint:

1. *Chinese Tag.* You must hold the place where you were tagged.
2. *Around the World.* In this basketball game, you must shoot from a series of specified locations.
3. *Jacks.* The ball can only bounce once.
4. *Simon Says.* You can only move when Simon says.
5. *Hopscotch.* You can't touch a line.

The above may seem to be merely rules of the game; nevertheless, they make games successful. They are constraints placed on otherwise open activities. The use of constraints seems natural in games, but it is also a principle of motivation that can be applied to many areas of teaching to make activities more enjoyable and to increase student participation.

ITEM 37. Movement Exploration

In movement exploration each child is challenged to respond to a given direction in any way he can. A variety of equipment can be used. For example, the following challenges have been used with hula hoops:

1. Roll it around the path and, when I blow the whistle, set it down inside the circle facing me.
2. How fast can you run around your hoop? (Try it three times.)
3. Can you run around the hoop and keep a hand inside the hoop?

4. Can you run around the hoop with both hands inside the hoop?

5. Can you walk around in this area without touching anyone or a hoop?

6. Can you reach down and pick up the hoop without bending your knees?

7. Can you move the hoop around your waist?

8. Can you move the hoop around your arm?

9. Can you move the hoop around your neck?

10. Can you move the hoop around another part of your body?

11. How high can you stretch with the hoop held above your head?

12. Can you hold the hoop above your head and drop it so that it hits the ground without touching your body?

13. Can you use your hoop like a jump rope?

14. When I blow my whistle, see if you can run to another hoop without touching anyone.

The equipment doesn't have to be elaborate. For example, a wad of paper could be used with the following challenges:

1. Can you slide the wad of paper around the room using only one foot? Can you do it going backwards?

2. Can you hold the paper between two parts of your body and move about the room? Can you use different parts of your body?

3. Can you throw it up in the air and catch it?

4. Can you throw it up and catch it in a different way?

5. Can you move sideways, keeping it between your feet? Under a foot?

These challenges are open-ended in that there is no one correct way to perform the stunt. They also illustrate the use of constraints to channel and motivate the students.

The movement exploration strategy can be adapted to other areas of the curriculum.

Math

1. Can you develop a series of numbers that are odd but evenly spaced? (3, 5, 7, 9, . . .; 101, 201, 301, . . .)

2. Can you make a triangle with a perimeter of 23 inches? Can you make a different one that still has a perimeter of 23 inches? Can you make a rectangle that has a perimeter of 23 inches?

Word Study

1. Can you think of a word that has a long vowel sound and names an action? (bite, smile, blow ...)
2. Can you think of two proper nouns that rhyme? Can you think of a pair of rhyming adjectives that begin with the initial consonant B, G, or L? (biting, gliding ...)

ITEM 38. The Area Code Problem

The telephone company uses a three-place number for the area code. If all ten digits (0, 1, 2, 3, 4, 5, 6, 7, 8, 9) could be used in each position, how many different area codes could be generated?

This is an interesting problem which could be presented to a class or a small group of students. Time should be allowed for students to examine the problem and to develop organized methods of reaching a solution. The correct solution is not as important as the process of developing an organized method of arriving at the solution. The goal is for the students to feel confident in their solution. "For sure" is stressed. That is, the student has developed a system and is confident that his answer is right. What are the possible number of combinations? A student could develop a system that would start 001, 002, 003, 004, 005, etc. Thus, he would have an organized logical solution and would be confident of his answer, 999. The fact that his answer is wrong (he overlooked 000) does not negate the desired learning. The object was to have the student develop a systematic, mathematical approach to solving a problem. You want students to trust their thinking.

By adding constraints you can develop a host of problems which students could work independently or in small groups.

Constraints for the area code problem would include the following:

1. The telephone company doesn't use zero (0) in the initial place because you would get the operator. Without using a zero in the initial position, how many different area codes could be generated?
2. The telephone company only uses 0 and 1 in the second position (3*1*9 or 3*0*9). (*This helps to identify area codes.*

Also, prefixes on regular phone numbers do not use 0 or 1 in the second position—338-2983.) How many area codes could be generated if only 0 and 1 can be used in the second position? What if only 1 could be used in the second position? What if only even numbers could be used in the second position?

The purpose of this example is to illustrate that you can get more mileage out of an activity by the addition of constraints. Students could develop their own problems and have classmates try to solve them. These activities will motivate many students, but the teacher is in a vulnerable position because the answers are not known. They must be logically demonstrated.

PRINCIPLE: **Teacher vulnerability increases learning potential.**

Learning opportunities are richer for children when they are not restricted to those things which the teacher knows. A teacher, by making himself vulnerable, can open the door to a vast array of interesting problems, activities, and investigations having considerable student appeal.

A similar series of problems could be developed for use at the primary level with a unit on money. How many different combinations of coins could be used to make 30 cents?

Solutions:

30 pennies

25 pennies and 1 nickel

20 pennies and 2 nickels

20 pennies and 1 dime

15 pennies and 3 nickels

Constraints:

1. You cannot use more than 10 pennies.
2. You cannot have more than 20 coins.
3. You can only use an odd number of coins.
4. You can only use two different types of coins (pennies and nickels, dimes and nickels).

ITEM 39. In and Out Machine

Present the problem shown in Figure 2-8 to the students. Ask them to raise their hands if they know the number that's going to come out of the machine. In the first case, if you call on a student and he responds with 17, he is right.

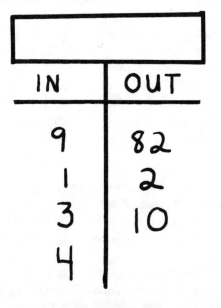

Figure 2-8

Ask him to put another number into the machine. He gets to call on the next person and tell whether that person is right or wrong.

When five or six students know how the machine works, fill in the formula that controls the machine in the box on top. In this case, the machine was operating on the formula $N \times N + 1 = A$, where N is any number and A is the answer.

ITEM 40. Word of the Day

In this activity, a student is selected each day to bring in a new word and share it with the class. During the day, the class tries to see how many times they can use the word. Each time it is used, a mark is placed under the word and, at the end of the day, the marks are counted to see how well the class has done.

Mrs. Sharon Nichels
Clarinda, Iowa

Comments: I used a similar activity and had trouble with it becoming too exciting. It's important to think in terms of an optimum level of motivation rather than a maximum level.

I had a large sheet of paper hanging from the ceiling to the floor. Each day we would add a new word to our list.

The word was presented by writing it on the board. It was also written on a 3" × 5" card. During the day, if a student used the word in the normal flow of discussion, he would claim the 3" × 5" card and take it to his desk like a traveling prize. Along with the card, he would put a star on his name tag for successfully using the word. At the end of the day, the 3" × 5" card would be added to the butcher paper.

At times, the traveling 3" × 5" cards and the stars made the activity so motivating that it would distract from the lesson at hand. When this seemed to be the case, or when I anticipated a problem, I would attach a stop sign to the butcher paper, signaling a temporary end to the activity.

Another problem with this activity was that I was using a competitive goal structure in which the students were competing to see who could get the most stars on his or her name tag. It is a good idea to place the marks in a common spot (for a cooperative effort) rather than on individual name cards. This changes the goal structure of the activity from competitive to cooperative. The class is seeing how many times they can use the word rather than acting as individuals vying in a win/lose situation to see who can get the most stars.

ITEM 41. Bunny Hop—Learning

An activity used to stimulate the dull, rote memorization of helping verbs during language time is the use of the "Bunny Hop" dance line. A list of helping verbs is written on the board for the children to copy and study so that they will have the sequence available. Demonstrate the dance, saying the verbs as you do each step. Then, add about five students for the first try, with the rest of the group observing. After going through the sequence with these five, another group is added. This procedure is repeated until all the students have joined the dance line and have moved around the room at least once. The following sequence was used: is, are, *has, have, had;* was, were, *has, have, had;* will, may, *has, have, had;* etc. Nothing is said on the kick to the side. Students enjoy this unusual method of learning.

Mrs. Robert Arthaud
Oelwein, Iowa

Other adaptations:

1. Learning number facts: 2, 10, *5, 5, 5*; 3, 15, *5, 5, 5*; etc. (In this case, we're working on the multiplication facts with five as the multiplier.)

2. Learning liquid measures: two cups *in a pint*; two pints *in a quart*.

ITEM 42. Individual Chalkboards

Each child has his own chalkboard, eraser, and chalk. They can be made from ¼″ masonite and chalkboard paint. They may be used for math problems, spelling words, or other drills. In this way, each child's work can be easily seen. The whole group can participate instead of just a few at the large board.

Ruth Noelck
Vail, Iowa

ITEM 43. An Arrow Story

Have your students supply the sounds for a story you read. The first thing you need is a cardboard arrow. This will serve as your volume control. Children watch the arrow so they know when to make a sound and how loud to make it.

no sound: ↓   soft sound: ↙   medium: ←   loud: ↑

Here's an arrow story to get you started. You'll be able to think of many topics for arrow stories. It's a great filler and the kids enjoy being actively involved in the telling.

"A wizard named Melsa lives in a high tower overlooking the Kingdom of Habadash. He knows only one spell, but what a spell it is! When Melsa *mumbles his magic chant* ↙↓   and *snaps his fingers three times* ↙↓ , he can change the weather. That's right! The wizard decides whether Habadash has winter, spring, summer, or fall!

"Now it's summer in Habadash. *Birds are chirping and singing happily* in their nests←↓. *Toads are croaking* as they sunbathe on the rocks↗↓ . *Children are playing* in the meadow↑↓, and the *bees* are busy gathering nectar from the flowers↗↓ .

"Then old Melsa *mumbles his chant and snaps his finger*↗↓ . Without any warning the *wind begins to blow*←↓ and a chill covers the entire kingdom. Snowflakes begin to fall and *the children and adults shiver* as they run home←↓. (They were dressed for summer weather, you know.) Once inside, they can hardly keep their *teeth from chattering*↗↓ .

"Now, the drastic weather changes were really not healthy for the Habadashians. Why, they practically all had colds! They'd *cough*←↓, *sniffle*↗↓ , *sneeze*↑↓ , and *blow their noses* all day long←↓.

"The seasons changed so often (sometimes six times a day) that everyone decided not to even bother going outside anymore. Parents looked out the windows and *sighed*↗↓ . Children *cried*↑↓ . Some people *slept* all day long↗↓ . And the dogs? They lay in the corners and *growled*↗↓ . Yes, everyone was disgusted about the situation.

"One day a *trumpet sounded* throughout the land↑↓ . King Herbert announced that everyone in the entire Kingdom of Habadash would march to the wizard's tower and tell Melsa exactly how they felt.

"Everyone wore raincoats and carried umbrellas because it was spring now and it was *raining*↗↓ . *Sucking mud* oozed all over, making it hard to walk↑↓ .

"When they reached the wizard's tower, the king stepped boldly up to the huge wooden door and *knocked three times*↑↓ . The *door creaked* as it slowly swung open←↓. The *bees* were the first to spy Melsa and they began to tell him how unhappy they were↑↓ . The *dogs* began to *bark angrily*↑↓ . Next the *cats meowed*←↓.The *cows mooed*←↓. Finally, the *townspeople* joined in↑↓ . *All of the animals and people talked at the same time*↑↓ .

"*The wizard covered his ears and moaned*←↓. 'Quiet! Quiet! What is it you want?' he asked.

"'You've got to stop changing the seasons so often,' said the king. 'Why, it's—it's—it's bad for our health!' and he *sneezed very loudly*↑↓ .

"'I honestly didn't realize how dreadful things have been for you,' said the wizard. 'I won't do it anymore ... uh, uh, I'll change the seasons only four times a year. Is that O.K. with you?'

"*Everyone cheered and clapped their hands* ↑↓   for they knew that life in the Kingdom of Habadash would be happy once again."

This idea was adapted from Brian Way's *Development Through Drama*.

Kerry Aiken
Tama, Iowa

SUMMARY

One of the best ways to stimulate student interest is through "hands-on" learning experiences. The interest generated is directly proportional to the relevance of the classroom to the real world. Having a cow lick your hand brings a different reaction than being told that a cow has a rough tongue. Examining the remains of an owl pellet fascinates and adds life to such concepts as predator, food chain, and ecological balance. "Hands-on" materials reach out and grab student attention. They spawn a variety of questions and help generate positive student attitudes.

Active student involvement can also be stimulated through the use of constraints. Constraints narrow the focus of an activity and increase its difficulty. When appropriately used, students enjoy the challenge presented by constraints. In some cases, when constraints are added to a problem, the answer will not be obvious to the teacher nor will it be in the answer book. This places the teacher in a vulnerable position. Reasoning, not the answer book, must prevail. This encourages student participation and opens the door to a whole array of new possibilities.

The successful classroom manager avoids discipline problems. One of the surest ways of accomplishing this is to actively involve your students in lessons they view as being interesting, worthwhile, and leading to valued outcomes. You should avoid using activities for activity's sake and you should avoid over-motivating. The activities in this chapter involve students in an active manner, providing a fresh alternative to worksheets and end-of-chapter questions. They help develop positive attitudes which lead to better cooperation and fewer management problems.

3

Providing a Varied
and Stimulating Atmosphere

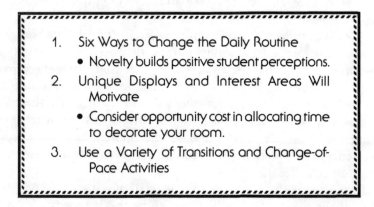

1. Six Ways to Change the Daily Routine
   - Novelty builds positive student perceptions.
2. Unique Displays and Interest Areas Will Motivate
   - Consider opportunity cost in allocating time to decorate your room.
3. Use a Variety of Transitions and Change-of-Pace Activities

SIX WAYS TO CHANGE THE DAILY ROUTINE

Variety adds spice; the unique and different motivate. We all enjoy the change in the daily schedule, a new seating arrangement, a new learning experience. *Novelty motivates.*

It's important to remember that novelty, in and of itself, won't result in better class management. Novelty has a temporal effect; however, if it is well timed, it can be an effective tool in building positive student perceptions.

PRINCIPLE: **Novelty builds positive student perceptions.**

ITEM 44. A Silent Work Period

A silent work period can be used occasionally to add a little spice and variety to your regular schedule. For example, you could prepare a ditto which reads as follows:

Directions: This is a Silent Work Period. See if you can finish without talking to anyone.

Go to the reading table and pick up the worksheet for your reading group. When you finish this worksheet, place it on the chair to the left of my desk. Be sure to get a drink on your way back to your seat.

Now you are ready for your English assignment. Pretend that you are a leprechaun. Write a story telling about your adventures as a leprechaun. When you finish your story, go over to the southeast window and get a piece of drawing paper. Skip back to your seat. Now draw a picture of you as a leprechaun. Be sure to color your picture. Put your completed story and picture on the west bulletin board for others to share.

Jog back to your seat. Before sitting down, touch your toes three times.

This ends the assignment. If you have completed it without talking to anyone, add your name to the Silent Squad List on the north blackboard and report to the teacher for your next mission.

Mrs. Barbara Sweat
Fort Dodge, Iowa

ITEM 45. A Half Day at a Time

Occasionally, make plans with your children for a half day at a time. Plan a series of independent activities, provide a vehicle for students to seek help if they need it, and supply the necessary materials and directions to allow children to pass from one area of study to another without interruption.

ITEM 46. Schedule Roulette

List your subjects on slips of paper and pull out a slip each period to see what will be studied during that period. You will need to keep special subjects at their appropriate times, but the change in the regular class periods can add a little excitement. To encourage students to follow directions and class standards, tell the students you will add an extra "Free Time" slip to the pot when they have been very cooperative.

The same idea can be used to decide what game will be played at recess with the class equipment. Have the class list about five choices. Every morning, the monitor pulls out a slip to decide the recess activities for the day.

Mrs. Madelene Moore
Anita, Iowa

ITEM 47. Martian Day

To add some spice, designate a day as Martian Day. All teachers and students come in costume. Eyes can be taped onto your forehead, large construction paper ears can be added as extensions, pipe cleaners with construction paper circles can be clipped into the hair as antennas, and funny hats can be made by covering old hats with tin foil and adding appropriate details.

Each student invents a special noise and has to make the sound whenever he moves.

Students draw monsters and add them to a Monster Wall. Cupcakes are decorated in Martian style. Of course, appropriate noises have to be made while eating the cupcakes.

The next day, you can write a language experience story to relive the fun of Martian Day.

Nancy Walden
Iowa City, Iowa

ITEM 48. Mascot for a Day

Each student brings a stuffed animal mascot for a day to keep on his desk. During language arts, draw the animal on manila drawing paper and color. Cut it out and trace another to make a back for the stuffed animal. Write an adventure story about the animal on the back sheet. Place the two papers together, stuff tissues between them and staple around the edges. The animals can be pinned to bulletin boards for students to read during free time.

Shirley Hall
Tama, Iowa

ITEM 49. Quiet Time

Explain to the class that there will be a special time every day during which the room will be absolutely quiet. Emphasize that no one can talk during this time and that you will be unavailable for help or questions.

Make sure to do the following:

1. See that everyone has some assignments to work on during the quiet period. It's a good idea to list several options on the board.

2. Ignore people who raise their hands or come up to your desk seeking help. (Of course, if it's an emergency, you would expect them to talk.) Each time a student talks, respond with a set phrase, something like, "Adam, it's quiet time now."

3. Use the quiet period regularly for a set amount of time each day.

Tanya MacAloon
Highland Park, Illinois

I used a similar period to start each day. Students could sign up for help, and talking was permitted if I initiated it or if I gave permission for a student conference. The time was used for such items as checking on late assignments, reviewing individual behavior contracts, assigning or checking special projects, and giving directions to monitors.

Comments: The unique and different motivate. Variety serves a purpose in terms of classroom management. Careful selection and timing of unique learning experiences can add spice to the dull and routine. Such activities as a field trip, a silent work period, and a hat day can add variety and contribute to that certain flair that makes your class an interesting place to be.

Remember, if students want to belong, if they see your class as a desirable place to be, they are more likely to cooperate and follow expected norms and established rules. The unique and different have appeal, they help build positive student perceptions and thus help avoid unwanted conflicts and misbehavior. They help to capture rather than coerce.

UNIQUE DISPLAYS AND INTEREST AREAS WILL MOTIVATE

Displays and centers create interest, stimulate student questions, and make the classroom a more desirable place to be. In developing centers and bulletin boards, it is important to consider the opportunity cost in terms of your time. Room decor can take an exorbitant amount of a teacher's time. It is also important to remember why the center is being developed. Hours can be spent developing displays and interest centers which are designed for adult eyes to meet the teacher's ego needs rather than room management needs.

PRINCIPLE: **Consider opportunity cost in allocating time to decorate your room.**

Consider the following purposes in setting up displays and interest centers:

1. Stimulate student questions.

2. Acquaint students with interesting areas of content normally omitted in the traditional curriculum.

3. Use novelty and uniqueness to build a desire to belong: "I want to be a member of this class because it is an interesting place to be."

ITEM 50. The Take-Apart Center

This center is set up to do exactly what it says: take things apart. Students enjoy taking things apart to see what they look like inside and how they work. (Caution: Many items, such as fluorescent tubes, can be hazardous. You should check with a knowledgeable source before taking a questionable item apart.)

If you use a letter such as the one in Figure 3-1 to ask for donations, an interesting assortment of gadgets and machinery can be collected.

Dear Parents:

We are developing a new interest center in our class. We call it the "Take-Apart Center." So far we have disassembled an old stuffed chair and a broken aquarium pump.

At Open House, we will display drawings and descriptions of the interesting things we have learned.

Do you have any gadgets, machines, or items that you could donate to our center? We would appreciate any contributions.

Sincerely,

Mr. Smith's 5th Grade Class
Steven Clark, Secretary

Figure 3-1

ITEM 51. Ceiling Hangs

The unique and the novel can make your room more interesting. Crepe paper streamers, with snowflakes or similar designs cut out and attached, can be hung from the ceiling to make "mini-partitions" (see Figure 3-2).

Hanging sheets of butcher paper can also be used to mark off

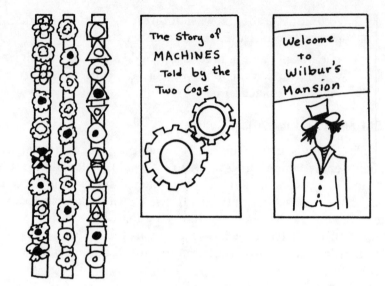

Figure 3-2

interest centers and study areas, or they can be used as backdrops for class presentations.

ITEM 52. The Maze Board

John Hull has a series of books called *The Maze Craze Series*, published by Troubador Press, Inc., which can be used to develop interesting centers. By using the overhead (see Item 17), an appealing and interesting bulletin board can be made by enlarging one of the mazes. Students could design their own collection of mazes and perhaps trade them with another class or give them to the children's ward in a nearby hospital.

ITEM 53. Monthly Pictures

In older buildings, the area above the chalkboard is a troublesome one to decorate or use effectively. One idea, pictured in Figure 3-3, that captured student and parent interest was the addition of a monthly picture taken with a Polaroid camera.

ITEM 54. Climbing the Mountain

Make a large construction paper mountain. Near the bottom of the mountain put the name of the coming month, and at the top

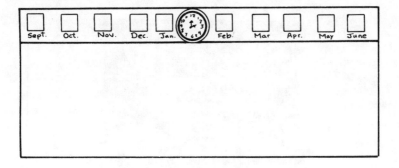

Figure 3-3

place the next month. Title the board, "Climb the Mountain." Write questions on index cards for each day of the coming month and arrange them in a winding path going up the mountain. A variety of questions should be used, including riddles, word definitions, recent sports happenings, and facts about our country. Of course, this could be adapted to most subjects. Have a little mountain goat climb the mountain, stopping at each designated day. On the back of the index cards write the answer for each question. After the children go home, turn over the day's card. The next morning, the children can check the answer and read the next question.

Mrs. Linda Awe
Algona, Iowa

ITEM 55. Visual Aids for the Music Teacher

The visual aids pictured in Figure 3-4 can serve as classroom teaching materials. Hang these as charts or mobiles. Laminate them to preserve them longer. Construct them out of colored tagboard. Hang the mobiles with monofilament fishing line and place gummed cloth picture hangers on the backs of the charts.

Donna Williams
Cedar Rapids, Iowa

ITEM 56. The Chalk Table

An old wooden table, or a piece of plywood fastened to a pair of sawhorses, can be resurfaced with slate paint (available in liquid or spray form from most hardware stores or school supply companies). One coating should last for the school year and the area can easily be redone the next year.

Figure 3-4

The children will enjoy sitting around the table doing their "board work."

Margaret Boggard
Clinton, Iowa

Comments: *This section presents a number of special displays and interest areas that can be used to provide a varied, stimulating atmosphere. The underlying strategy deals with student perception. If students see your classroom as having appeal, and cosmetic appeal can have an enticing effect, your students will feel good about being members of your class. They will want to belong and, thus, they will be more likely to cooperate with standards and class norms. The special displays add*

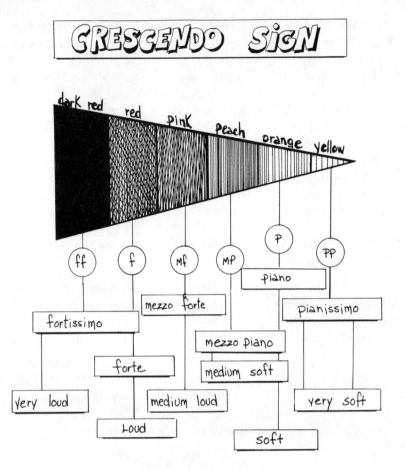

Figure 3-4 (cont'd)

cosmetic appeal. They can entice; however, consider the opportunity cost in terms of the time it takes to develop displays. Note that most of the items in this section are designed to be used for a substantial part of the year. I seriously question the use of teacher time to change bulletin boards every month or, worse yet, every two weeks.

A VARIETY OF TRANSITIONS AND CHANGE-OF-PACE ACTIVITIES

A main ingredient of any teacher's survival kit is a variety of games and activities which can be used at a moment's notice. What do you do with that extra 15 minutes when the bulb on the projector blows? What happens when students finish your beautiful activity in two minutes and you had planned it for twenty? How do you keep the lid on while waiting for the special teacher who is already five minutes late?

You need a host of ideas to fill the extra minutes that always seem to crop up. You need a number of change-of-pace activities to put life into dull, listless students; or, perhaps, something to calm them down. You need a variety of techniques for making transitions from one subject to the next or from one room to the next. This section provides classroom tested ideas that can be used to supplement and add variety to this all-important survival kit.

ITEM 57. Novel Way to Prepare Your Class for the Next Activity

The teacher says, "By the time I finish drawing (on the board) this cat (or whatever) and turn around, I expect everyone to have his math book out, opened to page 60 and be ready to listen."

This technique, as shown in Figure 3-5, can add a little spice and humor to your day.

Kitty S. Scharf
Montrose, Colorado

Figure 3-5

ITEM 58. Moving Young Children from Place to Place

In moving young children from one place to another, it is often necessary to have them walk in lines. Many variations in the way students are called to get into line can help instill the importance of being good listeners. The different techniques can also be used to develop classifying skills:

- All students wearing (*color*) socks get into line.
- All students wearing shoes that have to be (*tied, buckled,* or *slipped on*) get into line.
- All students wearing (*short, long*) sleeves get into line.
- All students with (*brown, black, blond, red*) hair get into line.
- All students whose names begin with (*a letter of the alphabet or sections of the alphabet*) get into line.
- All students who have (*number*) letters in their first names get into line.

Mrs. Flora Matthews
Miami, Florida

ITEM 59. Dismiss by Categories

The teacher names a category—flowers, TV shows, fish, animals with fur, etc.—and the students think of an item within that category. As their item is named, the students leave.

Mrs. Gail Reimler
Bettendorf, Iowa

ITEM 60. Sound Machine for Primary Grades

If you find your class getting "wiggly," just have them lie on the floor, close their eyes and make the sound of a barnyard animal, the wind, a thunderstorm, or animals in the zoo. If getting on the floor is too exciting, try having them put their heads down on their desks.

On different occasions have them experiment with such sounds as the following:

1. Typewriter
2. Water dripping in the sink
3. Bird sounds
4. Noises and comments that might be heard at a baseball game
5. A pot of water coming to a boil

6. Outerspace communication

7. Train noises

8. Making a sound when no one else is making a sound

9. The months or a set of math facts, letting the voice follow the teacher's hand motion

10. A car beeping its way through heavy traffic

Mrs. Lois Tschetter
Eagle Grove, Iowa

ITEM 61. Silent Math

Write a problem such as $2 \times \square = 6$ on the board. Hand the chalk to a student without a word. The student either goes to the board and fills in the answer or turns to the class and gives the chalk to another student. When the answer is written, point to the appropriate response that has been written on the board:

Yippee!

Oops!

Write another problem and continue the process.

Mrs. Norma L. Burleson
Wichita, Kansas

ITEM 62. Silent Math—Pointer Style

Write a series of numbers and operation symbols on the board as shown in Figure 3-6.

Using a meter stick or similar device, point to a number, an operation symbol, another number, and then point to the equals sign.

Turn and give the pointer to a child, who comes to the board without a word, points to the digits that make up the answer, and returns the pointer to you.

In return, you point to one of the key words—right or wrong—to indicate if the student was correct. If he was, point out another problem without a word and hand the meter stick to another child.

ITEM 63. Mental Arithmetic

Challenge the students to follow along mentally—no writing allowed—as you give them an accumulating arithmetic problem:

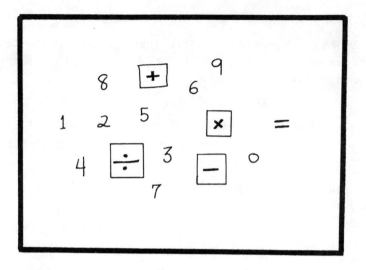

Figure 3-6

"Start with 5, add 3, plus 4 more, subtract 2, plus 6, times 0, plus 5. What's the answer?"

Vary the length of the problem, speed of delivery, and difficulty level.

ITEM 64. Adjectives

Hold up an object and hand it to a child. The child names an adjective which describes the object and passes it on to another child who names another adjective. The purpose is to see how many descriptive words can be named before a student gets stuck.

Kerry Aiken
Tama, Iowa

ITEM 65. By the Count of Five

Children are called on individually. They are given a letter and must name five words beginning with that letter in a given amount of time—by the time you count to five, snap your fingers five times, a pendulum swings back and forth five times, or a student finds a certain word in the dictionary.

Kerry Aiken
Tama, Iowa

ITEM 66. Listening Activity

When you have a few minutes to spare, pass out a ditto similar to the one in Figure 3-7, and challenge the students to see if they can follow directions. For example:

1. Make an X in the middle circle of each row.
2. Color the first circle in the second row blue.
3. Make three red dots in each of the circles in the bottom row.

Initially, you can give directions one at a time. Then, start giving two or three directions at a time.

Mrs. Doug Hill
Fort Dodge, Iowa

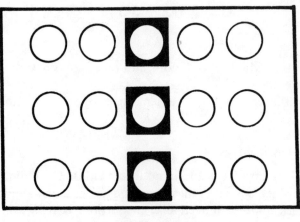

Figure 3-7

ITEM 67. Remain Standing, Please

Have the class stand and make a statement such as, "Your first name has two syllables." All students having two syllables in their first names should remain standing while the others sit down.

It's a good idea to make some spot checks to see if the students acted appropriately:

"Should Sam sit down?"

"What about Bernice, should she be sitting down?"

"Should Frank be standing?"

Make another statement such as, "You have one vowel in your first name." At this point, everyone should sit down because the first statement called for two syllables and this one calls for only one vowel. All students left standing after the first statement should have at least two vowels in their first name.

Listed below are some possible statements:

Set I

1. You have at least one pet at home.
2. You have a dog at home.
3. You have a type of spaniel at home.

Set II

1. You are wearing something with red on it.
2. You are wearing something with blue on it.
3. You are wearing something with two other colors beside red and blue.

Another way to use the idea is to have students write down the name of an animal on a piece of scratch paper and then stand. Use statements such as the following:

1. You wrote down the name of a mammal.
2. This mammal can be found in our state.
3. This mammal is not commonly found in a zoo.
4. This mammal lives in your house.

In each case, make several spot checks and take time to enjoy the humor of some of the possibilities. This is a good activity for getting acquainted with students and it is a good one for reviewing particular content.

Consider the following:

Math

Write down a number between 0 and 1000.

1. Your number is an even number.
2. Your number is divisible by 2.
3. Your number is divisible by 5.
4. Your number is less than 100.

Social Studies

Pass out an outline map of the United States and have the students select a state and write its name on scratch paper.

1. Your state is west of the Mississippi River.
2. Your state borders the Pacific Ocean.
3. Your state is south of Oregon.

Comments: This section provides a number of time fillers and change-of-pace activities. In terms of classroom management, there is nothing wrong with just relaxing and letting students use those extra five minutes to do as they wish (visiting, reading, or playing at an interest center); however, if the need arises and if conditions are such that you feel a structured activity is needed, there is security in having a number of activities in your repertoire to fill those unplanned moments.

SUMMARY

One of the most difficult aspects of teaching is the constant demand for new ideas, new activities, and new teaching strategies. When you are faced with seven or eight periods a day, 180 days a year, novelty becomes a real need for both you and the students. This chapter presented a number of ideas to add zest and novelty to your class. The chapter centered on the idea that classroom management will become easier if students see your class as a desirable place to be. If students want to belong, they will be more willing to cooperate with established standards and class norms. This will reduce the frequency of class problems.

Student interest can be stimulated through novel displays and interest areas. While the values of such items as creative bulletin boards and ceiling hangs are important, you should also consider the opportunity cost of spending considerable amounts of teacher time on room decoration.

The final area developed in this chapter was the value of having a number of transitions and change-of-pace activities at your command. A three-minute fun activity at the end of a difficult period of drill can help alleviate the pain and instill a positive student attitude toward you and the class.

Classroom management is a many-faceted concern. This chapter presented ideas for providing a varied and stimulating atmosphere with the goal of developing positive student perceptions. *If students perceive your class as a desirable place to be, they will be more willing to cooperate.*

4

Open-Ended Activities Which Keep
Students Busy Without Boring Them

1. Selecting Independent Activities
   - We must differentiate between our aspirations and our expectations.
   - Guidelines for selecting independent activities.
2. Thirteen Independent Activities to Try in Your Room
   - Open-ended strategies keep students busy while minimizing teacher involvement.
   - Use constraints to challenge and channel students during independent work periods.
3. Possible Game Strategies to Use As Independent Activities

INDEPENDENT ACTIVITIES

When you use a group approach in teaching a subject like reading or math, you have a constant need for independent activities.

As you work with one group, you hope to observe bright eyes and hard work among the rest. Realistically, in terms of independent seatwork, you'll settle for activities which keep the other students busy and out of your hair.

You can aspire to see your class totally involved, eagerly turning to independent seatwork as teacher directed activities are completed. Hopefully, the independent work reinforces ideas presented in class or has been individually prescribed to meet diagnosed needs. These may be your aspirations, but your day-to-day expectations must be more realistic.

PRINCIPLE: **We must differentiate between our aspirations and our expectations.**

One of the real threats to professional sanity is always knowing how to teach better. You can think of needed seatwork tailored to prescribed needs, but the reality of teaching prescribes that you work within many constraints: time, lack of materials, lack of support personnel, etc. To keep your sanity and to avoid the weakening effects of guilt, you must differentiate between your aspirations and your expectations.

The following set of guidelines provides healthy criteria for selecting independent activities.

GUIDELINES FOR SELECTING INDEPENDENT ACTIVITIES

1. Activities Which Provide Reinforcement for a Diagnosed Need

The ideal is seatwork based on diagnosed needs. You have diagnosed the student needs and have provided needed remediation. You provide activities which have a narrow focus and meet the essentials of good drill:

- The material is self-correcting or, in some way, provides immediate feedback to the student.
- If repetition is involved, measures are taken to insure that the student knows the procedures involved: "Repetition makes permanent, not perfect."
- Stress is placed on overlearning. The material is practiced up to the point at which improvement is no longer made. This is particularly important with low ability students.

2. Activities Which Provide Enrichment

The second criterion in selecting independent work is to pick activities which introduce students to new areas of interest or combine previously learned concepts and skills in unique ways. In some cases, the activities will deal directly with the curriculum. In others, the activities will only meet the criterion of being interesting to students.

3. Busywork

The third and least desirable criterion used to select activities is busywork, work that keeps the students busy and out of the teacher's hair. This is a weak criterion for selecting activities but a legitimate one. The percentage of activities classified as busywork should be small. Busywork is legitimate but should not be a mainstay of your trade.

Comments: There is no question that the amount of time spent in direct instruction in areas of need is directly related to student achievement. And there is no question that as students realize they are learning, management problems decrease. But, with the present support systems (availability of individualized instructional materials, self-paced kits, aides to monitor student work, space, etc.), there is a definite limit to the amount of diagnostic/prescriptive independent work a teacher can provide.

We should not feel guilty about using independent work which meets only the criterion of student interest.

Teachers need to be free to interact and instruct individuals and small groups. It is unrealistic to expect teachers to provide seatwork which is always tailored to individual student needs; thus, for the sake of effective management, high interest activities should be used in lieu of busywork. Much of the workbook and ditto work currently being used as seatwork represents busywork. It does not have a narrow focus and does not meet a diagnosed need. Furthermore, it presents a problem in terms of correction.

Open-ended, high interest, independent activities do not require a great deal of teacher correction and, yet, they keep students busy without fostering negative side reactions. The fact that they do not need correction avoids the negative feelings of guilt aroused in the teacher by piles of uncorrected papers, papers thrown out, or papers dutifully corrected at the expense of other personal interests and responsibilities.

We should aspire to always use meaningful seatwork. But we should expect to fall back on independent activities which merely involve students. Open-ended, high interest activities which require a minimum of teacher direction and little, if any, teacher correction, play an important role in classroom management.

OPEN-ENDED STRATEGIES WHICH MOTIVATE STUDENTS

You have probably experienced the frustration of spending several hours preparing a beautiful activity only to watch the students complete it in five or six minutes. There you stand, amazed at the lack of appreciation and sensitivity for your fine work, wondering how you're going to keep the students busy for the rest of the period.

The inappropriate use of closed questions is often the main culprit in such a situation. Closed questions call for short, predictable answers. They have their use as a diagnostic tool or in a rapid fire drill, but questions which elicit predetermined answers, usually one or two words in length, will not keep students occupied for very long. If independent activities are being used to free the teacher, closed questions are self-defeating.

PRINCIPLE: **Open-ended strategies keep students busy while minimizing teacher involvement.**

Independent activities should encourage student involvement. You want activities which are enriching in that students can run with them, run at their own speed and down their own paths. What is needed is a variety of activities which students enjoy and which permit them to work at their own level for an extended period of time. Open activities provide room for students to seek their own levels. For example, if you ask a student to list as many words as he can which have two or more syllables and which can be associated with dungeons and dragons, one student may generate five or six while another may list twenty. The openness allows students to seek their own levels. Too often, the usual assignment merely asks the student to answer a series of closed questions or match vocabulary. This holds all students to the same standard, blocking the ones who are able and frustrating many others. The time you spend preparing and correcting such worksheets could be better spent in locating or developing open-ended activities. The following item can be used as is or adapted to create a number of independent activities.

ITEM 68. War

This item was developed from suggestions made by Moffett in the text, *A Student Centered Language Arts Curriculum, Grades K-12, A Handbook for Teaching,* 1970.

Perhaps, as a child, you played a simple card game called "War." This game can be used as an open activity to reinforce alphabetizing skills.

Number of players: 2 or more

Game objective: to get all the cards

Materials: a deck of 3″ x 5″ cards, each having a letter written on one side (see sample in Figure 4-1)

Procedure:

1. Deal out the entire deck, one card at a time, face down to each of the players.
2. Each player stacks his cards face down in front of him.

**ALPHABET WAR
CARDS (3 x 5)**

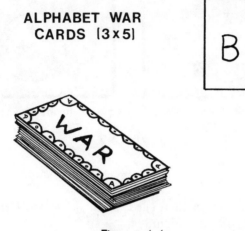

Figure 4-1

3. Each player turns over one card.

4. The player with the card having the letter closest to A (in alphabetical order) wins and collects the other "up cards." In case of a tie, they place three cards down and turn the fourth card up (this is called *war*). Again, the card closest to A is the winner.

5. The game continues until someone wins all the cards or until someone has won a specified number of cards.

This card game can be used in a number of different content areas:

1. *Telling Time*

You can make a ditto with a clock face and then run a number of 3" × 5" cards with the blank face (see Figure 4-2). Hands can now be added to each of the cards.

In this version, the student turning over the card that has a time closest to 12:00 is the winner. Using the blank clocks, you can make several sets, adjusting the level of difficulty with each set:

- Clocks that read on the hour.
- Clocks reading on the half-hour and the hour.
- Clocks reading to the nearest quarter-hour.
- Clocks reading to the nearest five minutes.

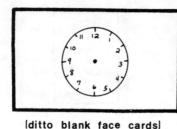 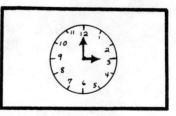

[ditto blank face cards]   [add hands to each card]

Figure 4-2

2. Largest Number

Write numbers on each card. In this case, the largest number wins. Some possibilities include:

- Numbers written in base five.
- Fractions (common and/or uncommon).
- Number facts (addition, subtraction, etc.).
- Roman numerals.

3. Longest Line

Draw a line on each card (see Figure 4-3). The student with the longest line is the winner. All lines should be approximately the same length. Use your ruler to see who has the longest line.

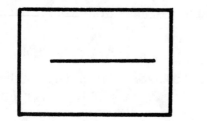 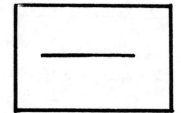

Figure 4-3

4. Indexing

Type a word on each card. The student turning over the word that would come first in the index is the winner. Make several sets, adjusting the level of difficulty:

- One deck with 26 words, each word starting with a different letter.

- One deck with 26 words, all starting with the same letter. In this case, students need to examine the second and third letters.

5. *Measurements*

Make a deck of multiple cards for each of the sets below:

I	II	III	IV
millimeter	milligram	minute	penny
centimeter	centigram	hour	nickel
decimeter	decigram	week	dime
meter	gram	month	quarter
kilometer	kilogram	decade	half-dollar
	metric ton	century	

6. *Officers in the Army or Navy*

7. *Cities having the largest population*

8. *Current standings in the National Football League*

9. *Presidents of the United States*

The earliest one wins. (For example, Washington beats Roosevelt.)

10. *Planets*

The closest to the sun wins.

In each case, make sure you have from two to five multiples of each card. In this way, you insure some Wars (ties).

ITEM 69. Webs

Challenge the students to see how complicated a web they can make. Give the students a large piece of butcher paper. You might consider a giant web with several groups of students building component parts.

Figure 4-4 is the beginning of what could be a very complicated web. Consider other main concepts for making a web: bicycles, school, city services, animals, disease, the eco-system in a pond, farm animals, toys, baseball, our state, TV programs, weapons, the post office, a grocery store. Figure 4-5 shows a web entitled, "Our Community."

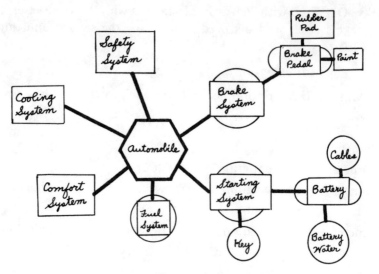

Figure 4-4

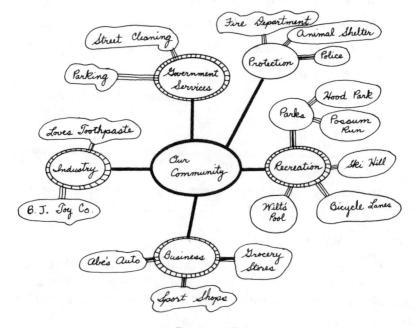

Figure 4-5

ITEM 70. Open-Ended Challenges

Combine open-ended questions with several constraints to challenge students.

1. How many three-letter words can you list which contain the letter A but do not have a long A sound?

2. How many fractions can you list which name a part of a whole smaller than ½ but larger than ⅛?

3. How many animals can you name which hatch from eggs but don't have beaks?

4. How many tools can you name which have a moveable part?

5. How many five-letter words can you list which are associated with economics?

By adding constraints to open activities, the students' attention is focused or at least channeled down a given line. Complete openness is often frustrating to students. They become worried and will ask for some type of direction or indication of what you want.

PRINCIPLE: **Use constraints to challenge and channel students during independent work periods.**

Setting constraints provides the direction by partially modeling what is desired. The trick is to design constraints which provide the right degree of difficulty so as to be challenging without smothering individuality.

ITEM 71. Classification

Challenge the students to see how many items they can add to the ones listed under each heading.

1. *Categories*

Fruit	Clothes	Vegetables	Sports
orange	hat	carrot	hockey
banana	shirt	beet	
prune	mitten		
	sock		

2. *Resources/Products*

Tree	Cow	Oil	Soil
paper	milk	gasoline	grain
toothpick		paint	sugar beet
lumber			

3. *Part to Whole*

Hands	House	Fire Protection
knuckle	window	ladder
finger	door	hose
thumb	nail	uniform
	concrete	boots
		badge

ITEM 72. Fold-outs

When the paper is folded, you see one thing (see Figure 4-6). But, when you unfold the paper, you see something else (see Figure 4-7).

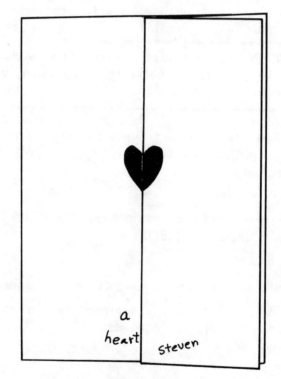

Figure 4-6

ITEM 73. Microscopic Drawings

In an independent drawing activity, use the constraint that what is going to be drawn has to be smaller than a penny. Given this

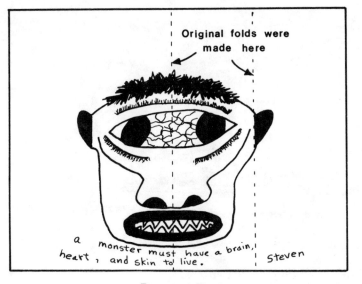

Figure 4-7

constraint and a piece of 12″ × 18″ paper, students can enjoy making magnified drawings of the head of a pin, a pencil point, a rivet, or some other small item.

ITEM 74. The Junk Box

A classroom "junk box" can serve as a good source of materials for art-related activities. By periodically sending home a request for materials, a surprising array of "junk" can be collected.

When given the restriction of using only the material found in the junk box to make a miniature sculpture, several students developed an interesting series of miniature motors; tongue depressors were used as the chassis, straws as the axles, and brads for the wheels (see Figure 4-8).

ITEM 75. Picture Cube Directions

Consider the possibility of utilizing a picture cube for directions. There are six sides on which to write directions and/or pictures. It's portable and can easily be set on a student's desk while he's working. It is especially useful in centers that are sequenced and need to be done in a specific order.

Stephanie Y. Norton
Rock Island, Illinois

Figure 4-8

ITEM 76. Lunch Box Centers

Students will really latch on to lunch box centers. Everything you need for the center is put into the lunch box. Send home a note to parents asking for an old lunch box, look for them at garage sales, or purchase new ones at a store.

These centers are portable and can be easily placed on a child's desk or shared between two desks. The boxes can be painted and decorated to fit the center or they may be used as they are.

Stephanie Y. Norton
Rock Island, Illinois

ITEM 77. Hanging Centers

Sometimes there are so many projects going on in a room that space is at a real premium. During these times, you can hang centers from the ceiling. As illustrated in Figure 4-9, use a cardboard box and heavy twine, and tie the box to an exposed beam or ceiling tile support. Check with the custodian to make sure that the support system is safe.

Leave one side open for storing materials or manipulatives as needed. On the three remaining closed sides you can put directions, a felt cloth for felt board, or large manila envelopes for holding materials. The bottom can be used for directions. Children are somehow fascinated by looking upside down to find directions.

You can capitalize on the novelty of reading upside down by taping the directions and required envelopes for a center underneath a table or desk. The students (first grade) lie down on their backs

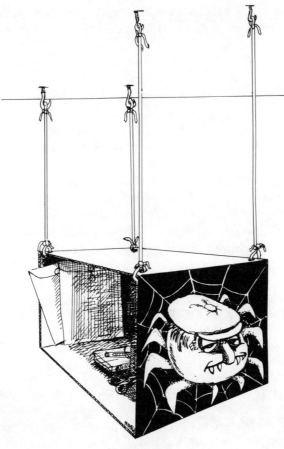

Figure 4-9

under the table and use a flashlight to read the directions. Keep a rug or pillow under the table for students to lie on. The flashlight idea makes it seem more spooky or detective-like. The types of themes that apply well to this center are the Halloween creepy critter ones, ghost stories, and code centers. The code centers are especially valuable because they can incorporate a lot of areas.

Stephanie Y. Norton
Rock Island, Illinois

ITEM 78. Traveling Magazines

Fill plastic vegetable sacks with six or eight magazines for every child. Include such magazines as *Ranger Rick, Boys Life, Young World,* and *National Geographic.* Selected comic books could also be included. Ask students to bring in their favorites.

Number each set. Every morning, rotate the sacks around the room so that your students will have a different bunch every day.

Mrs. Marie Cooper
Delta, Colorado

Comments: These open-ended activities involve the students. They keep the students busy without boring them. They don't create the volume of papers for correction that the typical busywork produces, and they allow the students to work at their own levels.

Constraints have been used with many of the activities to provide direction and to challenge the students. Many of the activities challenge the students to see how many items they can list. Fluency has been stressed because it is an important aspect of creativity.

POSSIBLE GAME STRATEGIES TO USE
AS INDEPENDENT ACTIVITIES

ITEM 79. Self-Checking Game Cards

Using cards, put the problem and several answers on one side (see Figure 4-10). Next to each answer, punch a hole. A student puts a pencil through the hole near the answer he thinks is the correct choice. The other students playing the game can let the player know if he is correct or incorrect. Put a star or some type of marking near the correct hole.

Nancy French
Davenport, Iowa

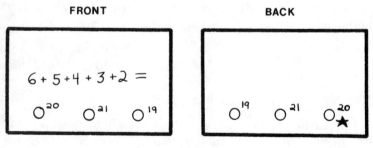

Figure 4-10

ITEM 80. Universal Game Boards

Game boards which have a variety of uses seem to be the most popular. Universal boards which are made by the teacher and then laminated can be designed by the teacher or fashioned from old commercial game boards. A possible format is shown in Figure 4-11.

These game boards can be utilized with any subject matter by quickly fashioning new game cards related to the current topic of study, such as capitalization, usage, math facts, or science terms.

If the rules are written universally so that the student answers the card and proceeds or goes back according to the response, even the rules need not be rewritten each time. Just a name change and new cards yields a whole new game for the current topic of study.

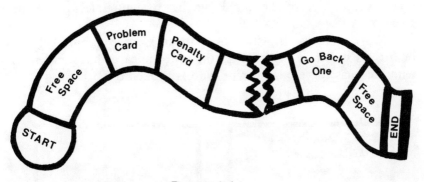

Figure 4-11

Possible Ideas for a Trail Board Game

1. *Include Problem Cards*

   Possible Rule: If you're right, you can roll the dice (or spin the dial) and move again.
   Possible Rule: If you're wrong, take a penalty card.
   Possible Rule: If you're wrong, you roll the dice (or spin the dial) and go back that many squares.

2. *Penalty Cards*
   - Go back three spaces.
   - You lose your turn next time.
   - Roll the dice and go back that many spaces.
   - You are stuck here until you roll a 6 or a 1.

3. *Free Spaces*

4. *Bonus Spaces*

- You get to roll again.
- Advance to the next Problem Card.
- You can move any player you want backwards six spaces.

Adapted from an idea submitted by:
Louise Burman
Burlington, Iowa

Other Game Board Ideas

Gummed stickers can be used to make simple game boards. The stickers are used as spaces on the game boards. You can tie the skill involved and title of the game together by your selection of the stickers. A few examples follow:

"Turkey Talk." Big stickers of turkeys are used on the game board. As shown in Figure 4-12, the problem cards have sentences with commas to help determine who is spoken to.

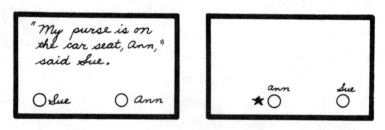

Figure 4-12

"Patchwork Puzzler." Large mushrooms with a patchwork pattern are used on the game board. On the problem cards, the student must select the item that does not belong in a list of things (see Figure 4-13).

"Flower-Flour." Use large floral stickers on the game board. The use of homonyms is the skill to be tested in the game. The student has to name and spell the homonym for the word given (see Figure 4-14).

"Happy Holidays." For this game board, use a variety of stickers. The skills questions deal with holidays.

Nancy C. French
Davenport, Iowa

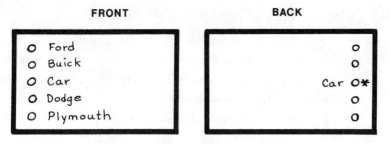

Figure 4-13

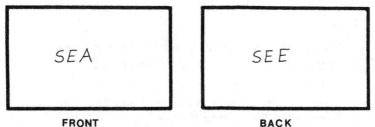

Figure 4-14

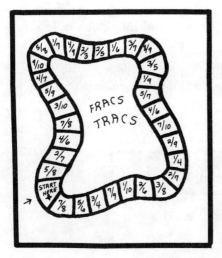

Figure 4-15

"Fracs Tracs." (See Figure 4-15.)

Materials:

Fracs Tracs board, dice, individual game piece markers for players, fractions bingo cards, cover objects for bingo cards.

Rules:

1. Four to six players begin on the start space.
2. In turn, roll the dice and move around on the track.
3. On your bingo cards, cover the fraction on your bingo card and read the fraction aloud.
4. The next player continues in the same manner.
5. There is no end to the track.
6. Continue going around the track until someone has gotten a bingo.

Variations:

1. If you would like to speed up the game, everyone may cover the fractions that everyone lands on.
2. Make the game more difficult by allowing students to cover any equivalent fraction as well as the given fraction on which the student landed.
3. The basic idea can be used with a variety of content areas. (*Homonyms*—*sea* on the track, *see* on the card; *Abbreviations*—*Street* on the track, *St.* on the card; *Fractions*—¾ on the track, and the sketch in Figure 4-16 on the card.)

NOTE: In making the Fracs bingo cards, vary the positions of the fractions so that all of the fractions will not be in the same space.

Nancy French
Davenport, Iowa

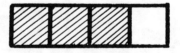

Figure 4-16

ITEM 81. Dot Dash

As shown in Figure 4-17, the configuration used in this game is a square with 49 dots in it, seven dots in seven rows. The object is to complete as many squares as possible by connecting the dots with lines. The players take turns, each one connecting two adjoining dots at a time. If a player is able to make the fourth line to complete a square, that square is his and he gets another turn. Each time he

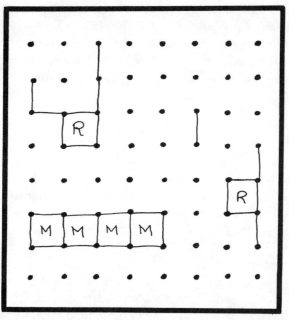

Figure 4-17

completes a square he identifies it by putting his initial in the middle. When all of the squares have been completed, each player counts up his score, and the one with the larger number of initialed squares wins. The important strategy in this game is to try to connect the dots in such a way that your opponent won't be able to add the fourth line to complete a square.

> *Comments: The games presented require little direct supervision. It's important to remember that games are not effective teaching devices for time efficiency, but they have a definite purpose in terms of motivation.*
>
> *With regard to the criteria for selecting independent activities, games are better than busywork because students enjoy them and they don't result in reams of papers to correct. This being the case, you should not limit your selection of games to only those which are curriculum-oriented. Generally speaking, a student can't play a game unless he knows the material involved and unless he has an equal chance to win (see Chapter 8 on competition). Therefore, in terms of the content, there is some reinforcement value, but the real payoff comes in the areas of social learning and motivation.*

Games such as chess, checkers, Pick-Up Sticks, Stratego, Clue, and Yahtzee should not be overlooked. They meet the criteria for involving students in an interesting activity while freeing the teacher to provide needed individual and small group instruction.

SUMMARY

Independent activities are a must for teacher survival. Your selection of activities should be partially based on this understanding. Choose items which involve students, and which require little if any direct teacher intervention or teacher correction. Don't limit yourself to content-oriented activities. Games like chess, Stratego, and Pick-Up Sticks have their place.

It is understood that the amount of time directly devoted to teaching has a positive correlation with student scores on achievement tests; however, it is also understood that most teachers lack the time and the support systems needed to generate individually tailored seatwork activities for all children during all their free time. Diagnostic/prescriptive assignments are highly desirable, but activities selected merely because of student interest have their place in terms of motivation and classroom management.

5

Helping a Student Develop
Self-Respect
and a Feeling of Importance

1. Demonstrating Unconditional Love and
   Respect for Students
   - Teaching success is based on unconditional
     love.
   - Successful teachers try to capture rather
     than coerce students.
   - The main focus of your self-analysis should
     center on pre-active decisions.
2. Methods for Getting to Know the Personal
   Side of Your Students
   - Respect is based on knowledge.
3. Using Student Ideas
   - Use numerous activities for students to
     contribute and feel important.

DEMONSTRATING UNCONDITIONAL LOVE
AND RESPECT FOR STUDENTS

Because your students are your students, you should have unconditional personal regard for them. They should not have to earn your respect.

Every class has a few "ringers." There is usually a class clown, a bully, a tattletale—a whole spectrum of characters. Some students will be difficult to like and some will be abrasive. You should expect these conditions and make the necessary alterations and effort to ensure that your pupils realize their maximum growth and maturity. You don't sit back and wait for them to be good or wait for them to conform to some preconceived standard. You accept them where they are and modify your plans and techniques accordingly.

PRINCIPLE: **Teaching success is based on unconditional love.**

Your students should not have to earn the right to participate in stimulating learning activities. This is an inherent right in any teacher/learner relationship. Interesting activities should not be withheld or made to be conditional upon "good behavior." A field trip should not be held off until the end of the year, used as a carrot or reward for good behavior. Field trips can be used early in the year to "capture" students, to show them that they are going to have an exciting learning year.

PRINCIPLE: **Successful teachers try to capture rather than coerce students.**

I'm not suggesting that you take a group of bulls into a china shop or a glass factory. You don't have to invite disaster, nor should

94

you hold back on effective learning experiences while waiting for students to shape up. Instead, break the task down or modify the experience so that the students can handle it. As I advised above, provide interesting learning experiences to capture your students rather than trying to bribe them into submission.

If you take an active approach and break the task down, trying to guarantee enjoyable learning experiences, you are demonstrating unconditional respect for your students.

If you take a passive approach and say that you'll only make class interesting if they do such and such, your interest in them is conditional. The fact is, you're really not interested in them, you're interested in their good behavior. As Fromm indicates in his book, *The Art of Loving,* "deserved" love leaves a bitter taste; *if you're only loved because you please, then you're really not loved at all, you're used.*

Don't hold back exciting learning experiences, waiting for students to "earn" them. Don't make your efforts conditional upon good behavior.

Certainly, you'll wait for your students' attention and you'll make some students sit out during an exciting activity. These are natural consequences of their behavior. Hopefully, in the future, necessary steps will be taken to correct the problem.

The key is to actively plan successful learning experiences for all students, not just the deserving and appreciative. *Students should not have to earn your respect and concern; it should be theirs unconditionally.*

PRINCIPLE: **The main focus of your self-analysis should center on pre-active decisions.**

When you think of effective classroom management, you should concentrate on pre-active decisions. These are the decisions you make prior to facing your students. You have more control over these decisions; you have time to consider and weigh the merits of alternative strategies; and you have time to seek out help and extra resources. When you concentrate on the interactive, the techniques for reacting to off-task behavior, you are dealing with symptoms. You are not in full control; you are reacting and not engineering. Real gains can be made if you zero in on the pre-active decisions related to building positive student perceptions.

Developing positive self-concepts should be a major concern, if not *the major concern,* of all teachers. We know enough today about the facilitating effect a positive self-concept has on learning and social adjustment to make it our number one concern.

Students develop their self-concepts as they see themselves mirrored in the behavior of others. The teacher who takes an adversary role with his students does little to develop positive self-concepts. Trust and unconditional love form the foundation on which successful classroom management is built. Familiarity with students is essential to this process. The more you know about someone, the more you respect their efforts. Keep in mind that lack of understanding breeds contempt and disregard.

As you learn more about students, it is easier to capitalize on their interests, to use and compare their ideas, and to give worth to their opinions and values. Teachers who use student ideas are more successful in terms of stimulating student achievement and nurturing positive student attitudes.

METHODS FOR GETTING TO KNOW
THE PERSONAL SIDE OF YOUR STUDENTS

It is very easy to be critical of someone or something you know little about.

PRINCIPLE: **Respect is based on knowledge.**

I can remember an incident that happened on the first day of school in one of my sixth-grade classes. The first day is always a beautiful day. Everyone is on their best behavior, you're fresh and enthusiastic, the kids are excited, and "cabin fever" is months away. At least, that's the way it *should* be.

I had started the day with spelling. At the close of the lesson, I asked the class to put their spellers away. In good teacher fashion, I glanced around the room and, noticing Billy's speller, I casually reminded him to put it away. It was all so innocent and "school-like" that I was stunned when Billy rose from his seat and growled, "You dirty S.O.B., I don't have to put my speller away!" Wow! The first day of school! It was hard to believe.

Billy was a difficult case. If I hadn't known anything about his background and his home life, it would have been next to impossible to work with him in class. But, as in many cases, knowledge of his situation made me wonder how he managed any cooperative effort.

Knowledge of the child's home life, interests, and values will give you a different perspective and help you to become positive and supportive. Knowledge about the student will help you to avoid dissipating your energies through moralizing or setting unrealistic expectations. Billy was a serious case; he had to be placed on Systematic Exclusion (see page 217); but, by the end of the year, he had rounded the corner and was experiencing positive growth.

The more you learn about your students, the more you'll understand and respect their efforts, and the more you'll come to see them as people. *Love and respect are based on knowledge.*

ITEM 82.   Invite a Student to Lunch

Invite a student or students to eat privately with you in your classroom. This special occasion provides an excellent opportunity to get to know more about the personal interests of your pupils. A sample invitation is shown in Figure 5-1.

Figure 5-1

ITEM 83.   Recording Student Interests

The more you can refer to student ideas and interests, the more you will encourage student participation. Try keeping a set of 3″ x 5″ cards handy to jot down individual interests as they are mentioned in class. Review these frequently to keep them fresh in your mind.

Ann Wright
Gunnison, Colorado

ITEM 84.   "Kid" of the Week

This activity encourages students to express positive, complimentary statements about each other. It makes it possible for each student to realize that he or she has many admirable qualities.

Each week a name is drawn from a box. The child whose name is drawn is the "Kid" for the following week. A sheet is passed around the room during the week and each child writes a sentence or two expressing something about the "Kid" that they admire or like. This is called "Filling the Bucket." On Friday afternoon, the "Kid" receives the letter and another name is drawn. Figure 5-2 shows a sample sheet that could be passed around during the week for each child to sign.

Figure 5-2

Another bulletin board idea is to use the caption, "All About Me." In this case, the child could display pictures on a timeline and include an imaginative look into his future.

For activities of this type, it is a good idea to send a letter home to parents explaining the project. A large manila envelope is helpful for each student to collect his treasures.

Another idea which can build parental support is a home visit. The special student can choose a day to stay after school and help. If the proper contacts have been made, you could end the day by taking the child home and visiting with his parents.

Another way to learn about the "Student of the Week" is to have a private interview with him over lunch (as discussed in Item 82). Using information garnered from this session, you could write a short story on chart paper and have it displayed, along with a snapshot, in the principal's office or in the hallway outside your door. After all the children have had their turn, you could type up the stories in booklet form. These make a nice remembrance to be given out at the end of the year.

Lois Terzis
West Des Moines, Iowa

ITEM 85.   "About Me" Bulletin Board

At the beginning of the year, introduce yourself to the class on the "About Me" bulletin board. Explain the purpose of the board and how it will be used throughout the school year. Send home an explanatory letter (see the sample provided in Figure 5-3). The rest is done by the children and their parents, with plenty of opportunities for teacher interaction. If a child does not bring anything, use a Polaroid camera to take a picture for display.

Dear Parents:

This year each child in our room will have a time to prepare a bulletin board about himself or herself. This will be coordinated with birthdays as much as possible, with summer birthdays filling in the "empty" spots.

The bulletin board may be put up on Monday morning by the child, or parents may come in to help. You may include pictures of the child, family, pets, etc. Any mementos that are personal to the child, things he or she has made or done, may be included. There is an extra desk by the bulletin board which can be used to display items such as models, collections, or anything you wish to show which would not fit on the bulletin board.

In addition, the desk will contain blank "Happy" notes, which others in the class may use to contribute to the bulletin board. The class will be invited and encouraged to add birthday notes, wishes, and happy thoughts for the child who is the child of the week.

Figure 5-3

Schedule:

Sept. 12-16	George Smith
Sept. 19-23	Alice Bishop
Sept. 26-30	OPEN
Oct. 3-7	Peter Bartley
May 15-19	OPEN
May 22-26	Marcella Washington

I hope that you will see this as an opportunity to help each child to feel good about himself, and that you will help your son or daughter bring in something personal when it is his or her turn.

Thanking you for your interest,

Figure 5-3 (cont'd)

Joyce King
Glenwood Springs, Colorado

ITEM 86.   Target

Have several students make a list of five successes in their lives. Items may include being an experienced bike rider, a good helper at home, or good at inventing things from scraps. Success in the classroom, at home, and in organizations can all be included. Each child then reads his list to the class. This is followed by having the class list descriptive words which characterize the student (athletic, patient, helpful, responsible, friendly, wise, clever, intelligent). These words are recorded on a target similar to the one in Figure 5-4. Students can tape their targets to their desks or add them to a bulletin board.

Linda Poppen
Algona, Iowa

ITEM 87.   Flowers and Bouquets

Have a flower base, as in Figure 5-5, printed on colored paper. Print the student's name in the center of the flower. Provide a box of colored petals. The other students each write something nice—an ego booster—on a petal and glue it to the base, making a complete flower. These can be used for a pretty spring bulletin board, or one person may be featured each day in a prominent place. Be sure to allow students to take their flower home.

Doris Davis
Crawfordsville, Iowa

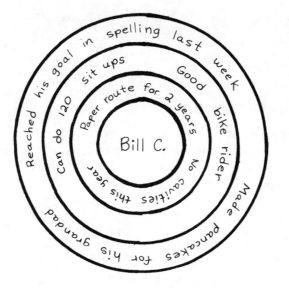

Figure 5-4

Figure 5-5

ITEM 88.   Family Tree

Have students bring in pictures of their families. Along with yours, arrange the pictures on a bulletin board with leaves, trunk, and a few little hearts. The resulting display is very interesting and informative.

Janet Peters
Clinton, Iowa

ITEM 89.   Feelings Chart

Clothespins with each child's name are attached to the little circle and can be transferred by the child whose name is on the clothespin to tell how he feels that day (see Figure 5-6). As their feelings change, they can move the clothespins.

Mrs. Jane R. McGee
Deerfield, Illinois

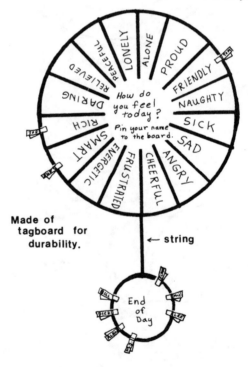

Figure 5-6

ITEM 90.   Am I Ready for School Today?

At the start of a week, a chart is made similar to the one in Figure 5-7. As the children enter the room, they put either a happy face or an unhappy face next to their names. This lets the teacher know how a child feels at the beginning of the day. It helps you, when you're working with the child, to get to know more about him. You may then be able to help with many problems, and you will have a happier child.

George Fraser
Opa-locka, Florida

☺	ME			☹	
	Mon.	Tues.	Wed.	Thurs.	Fri.
Carl	☺	☺			
Tony	☺	☹			
Joyce	☹	☹			
Mary	☺	☺			

Figure 5-7

ITEM 91.   Feelings Board

A bulletin board like the one in Figure 5-8 provides students an opportunity to express their feelings. Each child connects his piece of yarn to the different colored balloons according to his current feelings.

Mary Kurtz
Glenwood Springs, Colorado

Comments: *Students need to be recognized as unique individuals. Opportunities should be provided for you and your students to get to know each other. Respect is based on knowledge.*

Don't limit your recognition to academic work and don't sit around waiting for great performances. Instead, create numerous opportunities for students to share, to be recognized, to contribute, and to feel important. Respect for children is more than warm sentimentality. You need to learn as much as you can about each of them.

Figure 5-8

USING STUDENT IDEAS

The formal activities described in the previous section dignify students by focusing attention on their interests, their families, and their likes and dislikes. Generally speaking, positive self-esteem develops from interaction of a more subtle nature.

We learn about ourselves as we are mirrored in the facial reactions of others, the subtle nonverbal cues which tell so much. Being a "Star for the Week" will have a fleeting, negligible impact on a student's self-concept. What counts is the philosophy behind this approach. The teacher who is willing to devote class time to a "Star for the Week" will also take the time to encourage student-to-student interaction to give responsibility to students, to listen to children, and to acknowledge and use student ideas. It is the accumulation of these events over the long haul that changes a student's self-image. The big event can act as the capstone, but it's the everyday, common events which slowly nurture and build positive self-concepts.

You dignify students when you believe in them and in their potential. As you learn more about your students, you will be able to appreciate their uniqueness and their special qualities. As they become people in your eyes, you'll start to treat them with more respect and appreciation. These changed perceptions will shape your behavior.

It is hard, if not impossible, to control the nonverbal cues which leak out as you interact with others. These nonverbal cues are very important because they override what is said or done consciously.

Your perceptions of the students will change as you take the time to learn more about them, as you see the results of giving them responsibilities, and as you use their ideas and contributions. Consider the following:

1. Rather than quickly perform a little task, take the time to delegate the responsibility to a student. Try to be the greatest "do nothing" person who ever came along when it comes to routine room management. It takes more time and effort to delegate the chores than it takes to do them yourself, but if you delegate them, you're building a sense of trust and independence.

2. Have you ever taken the time to teach a couple of students a new activity so they can model it when it is first presented to the class?

3. Do your students help other students? Do you designate student "experts" so that students go to them with their questions rather than coming to you?

PRINCIPLE: **Create numerous activities that allow students to contribute and feel responsible.**

Be alert and seize upon these and similar activities that dignify students. In class, much of the students' recognition is under your control. You are the "Keeper of the Gate." You can be stingy or generous.

As you come to see your students in a new light, your perceptions of them will change. These changes will leak out in your nonverbal behavior and the accumulating effect of your changed behavior can result in students seeing themselves in a more positive vein.

Students need to feel respected and recognized as individuals. We can acknowledge many happenings, some of which are much more important than receiving 100 percent on a neatly written paper.

ITEM 92.   Record Student Ideas

During class discussion, record student ideas so that you can refer to them later. I have seen butcher paper and overhead transparencies used effectively in this manner. It is a good idea to develop a modified shorthand for quickly recording student responses. If you record the student's name, it is easier to give credit to the appropriate child in later discussions.

ITEM 93.   Group Captains

Divide your class into groups and assign a captain for each group. Captains are responsible for such duties as passing out papers, recording assignments for absent students, taking up completed work, and putting them into the appropriate tray.

In some special cases, the captains can be used as class experts as described earlier.

If you're having problems with pencil sharpening, they can also be designated as the only people who sharpen pencils. They can handle a similar enforcer strategy by being responsible for making sure that their designated work area is clean at the end of the day.

Adapted from an idea submitted by:
Ira Fisher
Opa-locka, Florida

ITEM 94.   Teacher for a Day

Give each of your students an opportunity to teach the class for a day. As you progress through the units during the year, those who choose to participate may select the unit in which they are most interested. They have to plan and carry through a lesson plan for one day pertaining to their unit, conferring with the teacher during the planning and execution.

The students will come up with many new ideas. At first, some students will be reluctant, but they will lose their hesitancy as they see others being "Teacher for a Day."

Mrs. Betty Parrish
Gainesville, Florida

ITEM 95.   Opening Exercises

Once a week, opening exercises can be conducted by a pupil who takes charge of the period, leads in the flag salute, and fills a ten-minute period with an activity of his own choosing. A list of suggestions could be: reading poems or stories, acting out proverbs, dramatization, singing, playing phonograph records, spelling bees, word games, location games, quizzes, and telling or acting out jokes.

The children will soon go far beyond the limits of this list. The initiative shows and the results are truly surprising. This activity develops a sense of responsibility, provides training in talking before a group, in giving directions, and in acting in an executive position, and also adds variety to school life.

Glenna Rhine
New Sharon, Iowa

ITEM 96.   Older Students Help

Children from another class can come to your class and help by monitoring learning centers and by tutoring individual students. An older student who needs to build his self-confidence might help by taking dictation, showing filmstrips, or performing some other support activity.

Older students could come twice a week at a set time and escort half of your class to their room where they play games or read for 20 minutes. They could help with difficult art lessons, such as carving Jack-o-lanterns.

Use special folders or spiral notebooks to communicate responsibilities or recommended activities to the students. You might also meet and have short briefing and training sessions with the students on a weekly basis.

Marie Smith
Anita, Iowa

You can pair your class with another, assigning several permanent rovers to act as substitutes for absent students.

Each child is given a set of flash cards on which to drill their partner. Rehearse the procedure several times. For example, a second and fifth grade class could work together. Set aside a ten-minute period right after recess. The students know which room to go to, half to one and half to the other. During the first five minutes, the fifth graders drill the second graders on their subtraction facts (alphabet, telling time, basic sight vocabulary); then, at a signal, they switch roles and the second graders take out their personal set of flash cards, with the answers on the backs, and drill the fifth graders on division facts.

ITEM 97. Big Brother/Sister

Sometimes, you'll only be left with nine or ten students after the band, safety patrol, and cafeteria workers leave. Have those remaining adopt a like number of students from a lower grade. During these off times, your students bring the younger ones to your class and learn new games, listen to stories, read to each other, go for nature hikes, etc.

Mrs. Madelene Moore
Anita, Iowa

ITEM 98. Snapshots

You can use a camera to make students feel important. Snapshots can add interest to autobiographies, they can give a personalized touch to the Job Chart, and they can be used to illustrate a class scrapbook.

Mrs. Mabel English
Clinton, Iowa

ITEM 99. Other Techniques for Using Student Ideas

1. At the end of a lesson, when the teacher is attempting to bring important points together in a summary, tie in points made by students in the class and state who said them.

2. Ask a student to respond to another student's idea:

- "Jimmy, what do you think of that?"
- "Mary, give us an example of Robert's idea..."
- "We have heard Ralph's idea; what do some of the rest of you think?"
- "Sandy, can you explain what Deb means by that?"

Here are five ways a teacher could use student ideas:

- Illustrate—"Give some examples for your premise."
- Validate—"What proof can you give us for your answer?"
- Expand—"What do you think could happen now?"
- Objectivity—"How do you think your answer is influenced by your own background?"
- Contrast—"How does your answer contrast with John's?"

3. Stay with a student until he has exhausted the idea. Ideas initiated by students should be followed up, and expansion

encouraged. Don't limit your response to, "That's a good idea." This brings premature closure in many cases.

4. If someone has a good idea while working on an assignment, have the child share it so that others can hitchhike on it if they wish.

5. Let the students submit questions for a test.

6. Use student ideas for free-time activities and extracurricular activities.

7. Use student-made games or puzzles for seatwork in various subjects.

8. Have students paraphrase directions. Ask a student to give an example to help clarify directions.

9. Choose a controversial or debatable topic and have panels of four or five children debate the issue.

10. Allow students to recruit other class members to help them prepare projects based on their ideas.

> *Comments: Using student ideas dignifies the student, adds variety, and provides an opportunity for students and teachers alike to learn more about each other. These happenings help develop a positive base which in turn discourages classroom management problems. Remember, the effective classroom manager concentrates on avoiding problems, rather than on techniques for reacting to off-task behavior.*

SUMMARY

Positive self-regard promotes learning. Teachers who believe that their students are good, who demonstrate unconditional love toward their students, who make a conscious and deliberate effort to learn about their students, and who try to involve parents in helping students to learn and feel good about themselves, are teachers who will be successful classroom managers. You engineer success, you don't achieve it by reacting. Skillful handling and directing of students won't do the job alone. You have to work on many facets. This chapter has presented a variety of techniques for (1) getting to know your students better, (2) ways to use student ideas, and (3) ways to make students feel important. Remember: *Successful teachers try to capture rather than coerce their students.*

6

Enlisting Parent Support

1. Ways to Involve Parents
2. Ideas for Improving Home/School Communication
   - You should have several contacts with parents prior to and after regularly scheduled conferences.
3. Seven Different Dimensions for Your School or Class Newsletter
4. Encouraging Parental Support for the Way You Correct Papers
   - Make sure parents understand how and why you correct papers as you do.
   - Self-analysis and clarity of mind are requisite for effective communication.
   - Time spent looking at right answers yields few positive results.

WAYS TO INVOLVE PARENTS

When you involve parents, you help students feel proud and you learn more about your students and their families. Parental involvement builds understanding, empathy, and a team relationship, all of which help to discourage the negativism and distrust that can quickly build up when people don't communicate. You can involve parents in a number of ways, such as the following.

ITEM 100.   Parents Help New Teachers Get Acquainted

Parents can volunteer or be asked to give new teachers a tour of the city or community. The parent could provide, as part of this trip, a short coffee hour with other parents. Possible community resources and field trips can also be identified. Parents can identify places in the neighborhood where their children spend time (Little League Park, creek area, hobby shop, recreation center).

Adapted from an idea submitted by:
Elaine Smidt

ITEM 101.   A Breakfast for Working Parents

Too often, working parents are unable to visit the school, so you can involve these parents by having a breakfast. This particular activity is aimed at the working parent. A week prior to the breakfast, each pupil writes a letter to his or her mother or father inviting them to a special event and asking them to come in their work clothes. A few days in advance the class prepares place mats, name tags, and table decorations. They practice how they will introduce their guests. At 8:00 a.m. on the day of the breakfast, children and parents arrive. The children assume the role of host and hostess by taking their parents' coats and making sure they feel welcome. Following the breakfast (which is kept to rolls, coffee, milk, and juice), the parents are introduced one at a time, after which they tell the children about their occupation. They tell what their work entails, the part of the job they like the best and least, the tools they use, and any other interesting facts. The entire event lasts a little over an hour. Attendance is usually near 100 percent, and feedback from the parents indicates they really enjoy being there. See sample forms in Figures 6-1 and 6-2.

Adapted from an idea submitted by:
Lois Tschetter
Eagle Grove, Iowa

EAGLE GROVE COMMUNITY ELEMENTARY SCHOOLS
Lela Howland

February 8, 1981

Dear Parents:

The second grade children would like to invite their working parents to a breakfast at the Lela Howland multipurpose room, beginning at 8:00 a.m. on Wednesday, February 22.

The major purposes of this breakfast activity are:

1. To help acquaint the children with the world of work.

2. To make the children a bit more aware of the various occupations in their own community.

3. To give the students some information about various occupations.

4. To help the children understand and begin to look at school as a place that can help them prepare for a job.

The second graders study the community as part of their Social Studies program. They learn how communities come into being, how a community is defined in terms of people, how a community supports itself, and the variety of needs in a community. To help better acquaint the children with this world of work and the division of labor in their community, we are holding this breakfast and inviting parents to attend, dressed in their usual work clothes, along with the children.

The breakfast will be rather simple, consisting of rolls, juice, milk for the children, and coffee for the adults. This will be served in the multipurpose room starting at 8:00 a.m. and lasting until about 8:30 a.m.

After the breakfast, we will all go to the classroom where

your child will introduce you to the group. You can then tell the children something about your job and what you do. Attached is a sample sheet listing the kinds of things you might tell the children. This classroom activity will last from about 8:30 a.m. to 9:15 a.m., at which time the adults are free to leave and the regular school class day will begin.

We realize that parents work at a variety of jobs and have various working hours, and that it will probably not be possible to get 100 percent attendance. However, we would like to have as many of you attend as possible if you are able to make arrangements to be here. Hopefully, it will be possible to juggle your schedule a little in order to be a participant. You might be able to arrange with your employer to get off for an hour or to have someone cover for you for an hour or so to allow you to attend. Only you will know your own situation and what you can or cannot do.

We hope to see you at our breakfast.

Sincerely,

Lois Tschetter, Teacher
Robert S. Wolfe, Principal

Figure 6-1

Please complete the form below, and send it back to school with your child on or before Monday, February 13.

Lela Howland Elementary School
1981 Second Grade Breakfast

(_____) YES—I will be able to be at the breakfast at 8:00 a.m. on Wednesday, February 22.

(_____) NO—I cannot attend the breakfast.

_____

(child's name)   (parent's name)

My Job

What is your name?
What is your job?
Why did you choose that occupation?

Figure 6-2

Was this your first job choice?

How many times did you change your mind about what you wanted to be before you went to work?

What do you do on your job?

Do you use any tools on your job? What are they and how do you use them?

What part of your job do you like best?

What part of your job do you not like to do?

What training and experience might help someone to prepare for this job (college, trade school, on-the-job training)?

Who depends upon your work (employer, people, family)?

Do you have a job where you have to be nice to people all day—even people who are crabby and ill-mannered?

Figure 6-2 (cont'd)

ITEM 102. Grandparents' Day

Set aside the day you introduce the letter "G" as Grandparents' Day. Send your daily schedule home and ask the parents to invite the students' grandparents or a grandparent in the neighborhood to come visit the class for all or part of the day.

Follow your regular schedule so that the grandparents may observe the regular routine. They will be surprised as they observe the difference between what children do now and what school was like when they were young.

Adapted from an idea submitted by:
Mrs. Pauline Ruebel
Barnum, Iowa

ITEM 103. Preview of What's to Come

Every Friday, the teacher sends the parents a list of the skills and concepts to be worked on during the coming week.

Mrs. Amelia Forgie
Green Bay, Wisconsin

A file of standard forms for sending notes to parents can be developed (see Figure 6-3). Consider forms for such concerns as:

1. Supplies the child will need.
2. Announcements of coming activities or study areas.
3. Notes requesting parents to set aside time for their children to practice a given skill.

HELP!!! MATERIALS NEEDED

The following materials are needed for: _____
(project or subject)

on _____ , _____
(day)   (date)

_____

_____

Thanks for your help!

COMING ATTRACTIONS

We are going to be studying _____
(project or subject)

next _____ , _____ . Please discuss
(day)   (date)

the following with your child:

_____

_____

We are particularly interested in learning more about:

_____

_____

If you or someone you know would be interested in sharing knowledge or ideas on this topic, please contact me.

Figure 6-3

Thanks.

Home: 362-9085
Work: 362-7564

Mr. Dick Shepardson
Room B.

STUDY PRESCRIPTION

We are studying _____ .

I need to spend _____ on the material
attached.

Other notes: _____

Student's Signature _____

Parent's Signature _____

Figure 6-3 (cont'd)

ITEM 104. Notes to Tell Parents What's Been Happening

Send a short ditto home at the end of each month. The note may hit only one subject area or it may touch on all subjects, listing what has been done. Here is an example for the kindergarten level:

Dear Parent:

During the past four weeks we have:

1.   Learned six new sounds and put them into words.
2.   Learned to say the Pledge of Allegiance.
3.   Practiced writing and recognizing the numbers 11-20.
4.   Worked three science experiments.

Some new areas to be introduced are:

1.   Addition and subtraction.
2.   Long and short vowels.
3.   Writing our last names.

Ann Wright
Gunnison, Colorado

ITEM 105. Daily Progress Report

When you start a new math unit, such as multiplication tables, send home a letter indicating the daily progress of each child (see Figure 6-4). This serves two purposes: (1) you can keep the parents informed of their child's progress, and (2) you can identify areas in which the parents could help.

Mrs. Joan Holmes
Waterloo, Iowa

Dear Parents:

During the next two weeks, we will be working on multiplication tables. Each day we will have a quiz. The children need a score of 100 percent before they progress to the next level. Your child will list the facts he/she is working on and will also record his/her score on the daily test. I will initial this entry and possibly add special notes about needed practice. Please initial this paper each night, indicating that you have had a chance to talk to your child about his/her progress.

Thank you for your cooperation.

Date	Area of Study	Test Score	Teacher Comments	Parent's Initial

Figure 6-4

ITEM 106. Friday Flash

Collect your students' papers during the week. On Friday morning, pass out all the papers and have them stapled together with a note sheet on top. Collect the sets of papers and, during the day, write short notes to the parents. The note sheet can be a ditto highlighting the week's events. Room should be provided for individual notes to be written to parents.

Parents know that the papers will be sent home on Friday afternoons, and they initial the papers and add any questions or comments of their own. The sets are returned the following Monday and collected. It is a good idea to save these for parent conferences.

This system encourages home/school cooperation. It also helps eliminate surprises that crop up at parent conference time or report card time.

Nancy C. French
Davenport, Iowa

ITEM 107. Parents Aiding Learning

A good way to involve parents, and also to get a lot of valuable help for the school and the students, is to sponsor "PAL Workshops." PAL stands for "Parents Aiding Learning." On the first Thursday of each month, parents are invited to come to school for the afternoon to help prepare materials. Teachers get various materials ready, such as letters to be cut, patterns to be traced, or centers to be prepared. All materials, with very clear and exact instructions, are placed in a basement work room. Parents, many bringing small children, come in as they can throughout the afternoon and prepare materials. The response is usually high and the finished materials are very valuable. It gives the parents a chance to feel as if they are involved in the educational process, and they get to see some of the things their children will be doing and using.

Louise Burman
Burlington, Iowa

Comments: Student attitude is shaped by your reputation as a teacher. The comments of older siblings, parents, and neighbors all contribute and will influence your success in gaining student respect and cooperation. You should consciously try to develop positive perceptions. Efforts in this area will have long-term payoffs.

The ideas included in this section can be expanded and adapted to meet your particular situation. Consider alternative ways to communicate with parents, to provide in-service for parents, to involve parents, and to enlist parental support in reinforcing basic skills and concepts presented in class.

IDEAS FOR IMPROVING HOME/SCHOOL COMMUNICATION

Perceptions are the key to solving problems. If you don't value the parents' role in the education process, if you don't actively seek out the parents, and if you don't cooperatively plan and share information with parents, then you're not realizing your potential as a teacher. Parents play a vital role in shaping student attitudes. They can fan fires or they can build trust and cooperation. You have to respect the parents' role, and you should become familiar with their concerns, hopes, and aspirations.

PRINCIPLE: **You should have several contacts with parents prior to and after regular scheduled conferences.**

---

1. How many parents have you spoken to before the first parent conference?
2. Have you talked with any parents prior to the first conference, about ways to enrich their children's strengths and natural gifts?
3. Have you asked parents if they have observed particular behaviors at home?
4. Have you checked with any parents to gather feedback on how students perceive your class, what areas they like most, or what types of student anxiety exist?

ITEM 108. Ideas for Successful Communication with Parents

1. Communicate at least one positive incident to parents about each child before the first conference.
2. Early in the year, at the onset of a child's lack of progress, develop a "plan of action" *with* the parents. Monitor the plan and provide feedback to the parents.
3. Make sure that the parents are aware of all the things you *can do* and not the things you *can't do* because of another teacher, the principal, or the lack of available materials.
4. Develop an awareness for the kind of information parents want about their children's educational progress.
   - Do the child's parents want an advanced listing of skill areas so that they can help reinforce learning at home?

- Do they want to know when their child is expected to bring something to share with the class?
- Do they want to know about their child's successes so that they can help reinforce desired behaviors at home?
- Do they want to know specific content areas so that they can enrich their child's exposure to those areas?

5. React to "difficult parents" in a positive, effective manner:

- *Hostile-aggressive parents*—Acknowledge feelings of anger.
- *Gossipy parent*—Change the subject to the child being discussed in the conference.
- *Overwhelmed parent*—Listen.
- *Punitive parent*—Emphasize the value of working on strengths and rewarding positive behavior.
- *Help-rejecting complainer*—Ask what he thinks would help the child.

Jan Cronin
Iowa City, Iowa

ITEM 109. Early Meeting with Parents

Have a meeting for parents during the first week of school. During the first week, students are on their best behavior, you are fresh, and parents are in a good frame of mind because their children are back in school. This is the time for a meeting. You can still plan to meet with parents at "Back to School Night" or "Open House." This early meeting gets things off to a good start.

Some of the items you may want to discuss at this meeting include:

1. Provide a simple ice-breaker for parents to get to know each other.
2. Items, such as worksheets, individual contracts, or report forms, that you will be sending home.
3. Expectations regarding children going out for recess.
4. Gym clothes and recess equipment brought from home.
5. How papers are going to be corrected.
6. How to handle homework and missed assignments when students are absent.

7. Expectations and schedule for students to share during current events and "show and tell."

8. Behavior signs to be concerned about and an invitation to call and discuss.

9. Your use of differential treatment and how to best respond to children who feel your treatment is unfair.

10. The daily schedule, the types of activities and curriculum areas you will be studying, and general program goals.

11. Ways parents can help enrich learning and classroom experiences.

12. Have parents fill out a card indicating when they can be reached and whether they mind if you call them during the day or evening.

13. Encourage parents to call if they have a concern or a suggestion for any part of your class or the school's program.

14. Help parents arrange car pools for rainy days.

This early meeting should be followed by several individual contacts prior to your first parent conference. The early investment of time will ease communication, relax all parties concerned, and help build positive team relationships, all of which will have a nurturing effect on class management and individual growth and development.

Adapted from an idea submitted by:
Jan Cronin
Iowa City, Iowa

ITEM 110. Guidelines to Help Parents Get Ready for Conferences

---

Dear Parents:

Here are some ideas that might help you get ready for conferences. It often helps to think of questions or concerns before you come, write them down, and bring them along to the conference. Here are some thoughts that might help you get started. Please bring your child's report card with you to your conference. Thank you!

My child has problems with ...

I don't understand ...

What can I do when ...?

Would pre-first grade summer school be helpful?

I like the way ...

Why do ...?

What does your child want you to ask the teacher?

Will your child be at Coolidge next year?

Other ...

Bring this and the report card with you!!!

ITEM 111. Novel Notes to Parents

As discussed in Chapter 3, the unique can motivate. A cleverly designed note highlighted in felt pens or printed on colored paper adds appeal to the family bulletin board or refrigerator door. We're talking about cosmetic appeal which is superficial but, as in all endeavors, every little bit helps. The examples in Figure 6-5 were used in a History Club.

Groups or clubs such as this can make considerable use of parents. Such groups may be conceived to run for a month or so, or they might be organized around just one or two special activities.

Lynn Nielsen
Cedar Falls, Iowa

Comments: *You can increase the benefits realized from parent-teacher conferences if you have a number of informal contacts with the parents prior to the conference (letters and notes sent home, telephone calls, small group meetings, involvement of parents in class activities). If you set the stage by asking parents to think about certain areas prior to the conference, they will come in better organized and ready to work cooperatively. If the parent doesn't know what the agenda or focus of the meeting are going to be, the likelihood of developing a defensive atmosphere is increased.*

SEVEN DIFFERENT DIMENSIONS FOR YOUR SCHOOL OR CLASS NEWSLETTER

The newsletter is a mainstay when it comes to communicating to parents. Calendars, notes, reminders, helpful hints, games, and

DUBUQUE HERE WE COME!

Dear Parent(s):

On July 6, the Iowa history group will be going to Dubuque to visit the historic sites in that part of our state.

We will be departing at 8:30 sharp and returning at approximately 5:00. Please be sure your child brings a sack lunch as well as a can of pop or a thermos.

Thank you very much.

Sincerely,
Lynn Nielsen

THE IOWA CITY EXPRESS

Dear Parent(s)

On July 18th, the Iowa history group will be visiting the Iowa City area. They will be going to the Amanas, Old Capitol, and Herbert Hoover's birthplace.

Departure: 8:30
Return: 5:00

Please bring a sack lunch.

Sincerely
Mrs. Lynn Nielsen

Figure 6-5

sample activities have been used to keep parents informed and suggest areas to be reinforced or expanded at home.

Does your school or class newsletter make use of the ideas illustrated in Items 112 through 117?

ITEM 112. Notes on Progress Being Made

Color Words

During December, many of the reading groups will be concentrating on reading and using the color words. We already have 35 out of 46 kids who know all their color words. The afternoon class will soon have their color word party.

The whole class will also be trying to improve their coloring papers. So, please be honest with your children about their work.

Thank you.

Lach Ross
Cedar Rapids, Iowa

ITEM 113. Encouragement for Parents to Help Their Children Learn Certain Skills

---

Boots and Coats

How does the teacher get all those coats and boots on in the winter? Easy ... I don't!! Your child needs to learn to get ready to go outside alone. That one or two minutes you spend to get your child ready adds up to about 15 or 20 minutes for the teacher. As a result, the children who can get ready by themselves will leave on time, the others may arrive home later, until they learn to master their own clothing. Thanks.

Lach Ross
Cedar Rapids, Iowa

ITEM 114. Enlisting Parent Support to Help Solve a Problem

Do parents realize how much food is wasted in the hot lunch program? I'm sure we here at school were not aware until we actually started to take a close look.

For example, one day we kept track of the amount of milk that the children did not drink. To our amazement, 4 gallons of milk were wasted. When one figures there are 20 other schools in the Iowa City system, the amount of milk wasted seems to be overwhelming.

A few of the schools took a survey of the most liked and disliked foods on the school menus. The information was given to the food service director in an effort to avoid some of the most unpopular items in future menu planning. No vegetable seems to be especially popular. However, there are certain guidelines that the school menus must follow in order to receive federal reimbursement. Serving a vegetable every day is one of the requirements.

We have not required children to "clean their trays," nor do we intend to require it. We realize that there are certain foods that some children dislike so much that they cannot eat them. We have tried a gimmick that sometimes encourages the younger students to eat a certain item. For example, we have declared that "this is eat your green beans day." When it is time to dismiss a table, those who have eaten their green beans are dismissed first. The others wait only 10 or 15 seconds more before they are dismissed, but the incentive is there to eat the beans and sometimes it works.

This has become a game and the children want to know what food item they have to eat on a particular day to be dismissed first. This works if it is not used too often.

Perhaps you, as parents, could help by checking the menu and, if the main part of the meal is something you know your child will not eat, send a sack lunch.

Wasting food is a problem and anything you can do would be appreciated.

Hoover Elementary School
Iowa City, Iowa

ITEM 115. Clarification of School Board Policy

Gift Policy

According to school board policy #1320, "Parents and students are to be discouraged from giving gifts to teachers." I

ask your help in letting me stand by this policy ... I receive
enough thanks by watching and helping the children learn
and grow.

Lach Ross
Cedar Rapids, Iowa

ITEM 116. A Suggested Activity to Use at Home: Kindergarten Newsletter

Bonus-of-the-Month-Club

This month's free offer is a game that will require some parent
help to assemble.

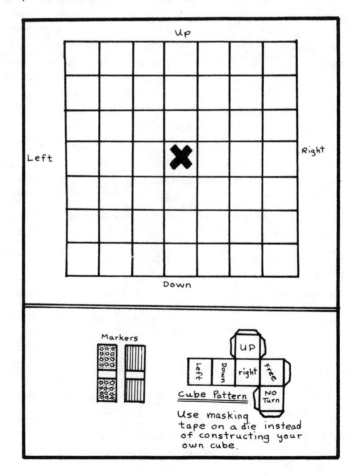

First, cut out and tape together a cube and two game markers.

To play, both people sit so that they are on the "down" side of the game board.

Place both markers on the "X" and start the game. Then, each player rolls the cube and moves only one square in the direction stated. A free move entitles the player to move in any of the four directions.

The winner is the first one to move off the game board. Have fun!!

Lach Ross
Cedar Rapids, Iowa

ITEM 117. Drill Activities for Parents to Use at Home

A Math Toy

This month's "free offer" is a flashcard game to help your child identify the numerals and the number words. The cards can be used in several ways after they are cut apart.

1. Count each group of dots.
2. Put the dots in order from smallest to largest group.
3. Match the numerals with the correct group of dots.
4. Put the numerals in the correct order (left to right).
5. Match the number words with the correct numeral.
6. Put the number words in the correct order.
7. Match the number words with the correct group of dots.

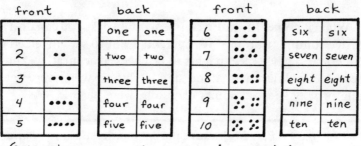

(Dittoed construction paper included in newsletter)

For best results, have your child master step 1 before going on to the next step.

It would be nice if the whole class could do all seven steps by the end of the month. That will take some work—so get started!

Lach Ross
Cedar Rapids, Iowa

ITEM 118. First Grade News

Beginning on the first day of first grade, write TODAY'S NEWS on the board. Start with the date and the weather. Those students who want to may contribute a line. You should record the student's contributions in their own words. When the board is filled, help each student read their own line. At the end of the day, copy the news, adding a few lines about activities in the class that day. Run these off each day and then collate them at the end of the first week. The resulting newsletter is sent home on Fridays as *First Grade News*. The children can take turns designing the cover.

You can include stories the students have written, a report on a field trip, a poem of the season, and other interesting items. On Fridays, read through the news together. Many of the parents will also read through the newsletter with their children. This activity serves two purposes: it's a language experience activity and it develops positive home/school relationships.

Dorothy Theobald
Iowa City, Iowa

ENCOURAGING PARENTAL SUPPORT
FOR THE WAY YOU CORRECT PAPERS

When it comes to sending home schoolwork, you can do a lot to improve communication. Most parents want to see corrected work come home. They expect papers to be checked accurately, and they expect their children to understand why answers were marked wrong or why specific points or grades were given.

PRINCIPLE: **Make sure parents understand how and why you correct papers as you do.**

Again, perceptions play a key role. If parents know why you have students correct work and if they know why you don't red pencil all errors, they will not react negatively and talk disparagingly about you and your program when they find unmarked errors on papers.

ITEM 119. A Rubber Stamp Designates What Elements in a Paper Were Checked

A stamp such as the one shown in Figure 6-6 can be used to specify what was checked when the paper was corrected. In some written work, you may only want to check the sentence structure. (Note: When the paper is stamped, a plus could be put in the circle to designate that this was the only area checked.) This way, parents will more readily understand why you did not mark every error on the paper. Furthermore, you don't have to deflate a student's ego by covering his paper with red ink.

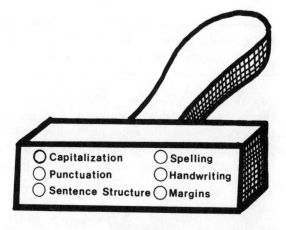

○ Capitalization   ○ Spelling
○ Punctuation   ○ Handwriting
○ Sentence Structure ○ Margins

Figure 6-6

ITEM 120. A "Student Corrected" Stamp

Some types of work are easily corrected by students. A math captain can be excused from math for a day or a week to correct papers.

When he corrects a paper, he stamps it "Student Corrected." The stamp in Figure 6-7 helps eliminate the P.R. problems that can arise if a student is careless in correcting work. And students love to use a rubber stamp!

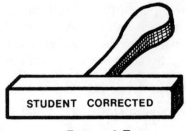

Figure 6-7

Research indicates that students who correct their own papers outscore students who trade papers for correcting purposes. Students who correct their own work also outscore students in classrooms where the teacher habitually corrects all papers.

If you take the necessary steps to carefully explain why you handle papers as you do, then you'll find that the parents will be accepting and supportive. Self-analysis is an important first step in this process.

PRINCIPLE: **Self-analysis and clarity of mind are requisite for effective communication.**

Have you ever questioned the amount of time you spend correcting papers? As pictured in Figure 6-8, I believe there is a negative correlation between the amount of time some teachers spend correcting papers and their general effectiveness.

The 15 minutes it takes to correct a set of math papers could be used to:

1. Analyze errors for needed reteaching.

2. Write notes of encouragement.

3. Tutor a child.

4. Assign a special project or help a student learn to use a particular resource tool.

5. Telephone a resource person and arrange for a visit (a pharmacist could talk to your class about the use of the metric system in pharmacology).

6. Call a parent to explain how well their child has been doing in getting his assignments in on time.

7. Make a set of problem cards or flashcards to use as a follow-up activity.

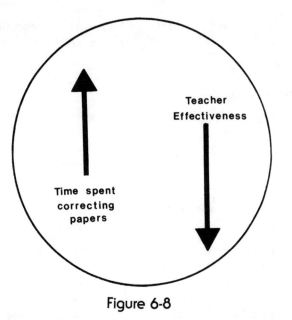

Figure 6-8

8. Visit with a child about out-of-school activities.

In other words, there is an "opportunity cost" to the time you spend correcting papers. You have used that time correcting papers and lost the opportunity to do something else. Every choice situation is a trade-off; with one decision you'll gain something and, of course, lose the chance to do something else. The point is, you should consider your alternatives.

In the typical spelling test, most students get at least 80 percent of the problems right. Considering the right answers may have some therapeutic value for you as a teacher, but you also want to look at errors.

PRINCIPLE: **Time spent looking at right answers yields few positive results.**

Your time should be spent looking at errors, trying to figure out what is causing the student difficulty. Rather than correct a set of papers, your time might be better spent writing notes or communicating with parents in some other way. Your time could be better spent tutoring a child or planning an enriching learning experience. Try to cut down on the amount of time you spend checking routine papers (spelling tests, math papers, worksheets).

This is not to say that you should cut back on time spent diagnosing problems missed and/or reinforcing students on routine assignments.

ITEM 121. The Slate

At the beginning of the year, ditto a number of grids similar to the one shown in Figure 6-9.

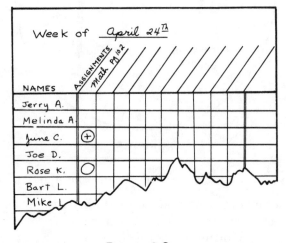

Figure 6-9

As each assignment is collected, it is recorded on "the Slate." If a student does not turn in an assignment, a circle is drawn in his or her box (see Rose K.). When that assignment is turned in, the student puts a plus in the circle (see June C.).

The class list or "slate" can easily be kept on a clipboard and left in one of the chalk trays. In this way, students can conveniently check to see if all their assignments are turned in.

These weekly forms should be kept for future reference and for student and parent/teacher conferences.

ITEM 122. Independent Workers

Students who work independently can use record cards that are turned in with their work (see Figure 6-10). The "Teacher Comments" column is used to provide feedback and keep track of student progress. These can be sent home to parents or saved for use in conferences.

DATE	WORK COMPLETED	TEACHER COMMENTS
2-18	Fractions 19-25	100% accurate and neat work
2-25	Fractions 26-32	Problems with common denominators
3-4	Fractions Test	-2 Good understanding Good speed

Figure 6-10

ITEM 123. Spiral Notebooks

This idea can be used with the whole class or just those students who need help keeping track of papers.

The student is required to have a spiral notebook for each area of study. All work assigned, other than dittos and special tests, is done in the notebooks. The paper in the spirals is not to be used as scrap paper, nor is any of it to be torn out. This should be made very clear. Each page is to be used, none wasted. This system serves several purposes: (1) It eliminates any doubt as to whether an assignment was completed. If the work was done, it should be in the notebook. (2) It avoids the loss of loose, individual papers. (3) Reference can easily be made to past work (Has the student been making progress? Is the student doing a better job of checking his work?). Again, these notebooks come in very handy at conference time.

Mrs. Jan Duensing
Carpentersville, Illinois

ITEM 124. Corrections Time

As children finish their work, they place it in their individual folders. The work is checked over during lunch or some other break, and then returned to the children during "Corrections Time," which is a regularly scheduled period late in the day. At that time, all errors are corrected, help is given to those who had difficulty, and the work is taken home. In this way, the child is given immediate feedback and goes home feeling successful. This also alleviates the problem of the child not understanding why he made the errors or not understanding why he received the grade he did. Parents respond very favorably to a child who has learned from his mistakes.

Dorothy Theobald
Iowa City, Iowa

Comments: *Early in the year, make sure you communicate to parents how and why you correct papers or have them corrected as you do. Consider which papers you'll correct, when students will correct their own work, when parents can expect to see papers coming home, and how concerns about corrected work should be handled.*

Students and parents talk about school at home. The more you structure that talk, the better your chances are that those discussions will be supportive and will be a factor in developing desirable perceptions about you and your class. Positive perceptions make classroom management a much easier task.

SUMMARY

Perceptions are the key to successful classroom management. Student attitude is directly affected by parental attitudes and neighborhood gossip. If you don't communicate to parents, then you increase the likelihood of misunderstandings festering into problems.

When you involve people, they feel ownership and they develop a personal responsibility for the success or failure of a project. This cooperative spirit, along with the potential for added insight, complimentary action, and extra help, can do much to make your teaching more effective and your classroom a more desirable place to be.

7

Developing Class Unity

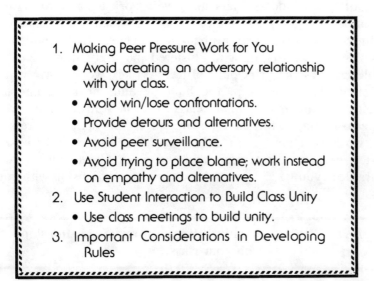

1. Making Peer Pressure Work for You
   - Avoid creating an adversary relationship with your class.
   - Avoid win/lose confrontations.
   - Provide detours and alternatives.
   - Avoid peer surveillance.
   - Avoid trying to place blame; work instead on empathy and alternatives.
2. Use Student Interaction to Build Class Unity
   - Use class meetings to build unity.
3. Important Considerations in Developing Rules

MAKING PEER PRESSURE WORK FOR YOU

Classes, as organized groups, will develop norms. The peer group will tolerate certain behaviors, encourage and reinforce others, and extinguish still others.

If, on the whole, you have a positive relationship with your class, peer pressure will work for you. This being the case, the more unity your class has, the greater the dividends in terms of classroom management. However, if you have an adversary relationship with most of your students, class unity will work against you. I can remember a tenth grade biology class in which the teacher was writing on the board, with his back to the class. All of a sudden, he was plastered with 11 oranges. Flustered and angry, he marched the whole class to the principal's office. As luck would have it, the principal was away from the building and the fledgling vice-principal was no match for the class. Not one student would point an accusing finger; the class was unified. In this case, peer pressure was working against the teacher because an enemy relationship existed between the teacher and the class. Class unity is only desirable if you have a positive, supportive relationship with your class.

PRINCIPLE: **Avoid creating an adversary relationship with your class.**

If you're trying to avoid an adversary relationship, the first place to start is with your program. Students need to see your class as a desirable place to be. The ideas suggested in the first six chapters of this book will help develop such an attitude.

Once you have a positive relationship with most of your students, class unity will work for you and you'll want to encourage it.

PRINCIPLE: **Avoid win/lose confrontations.**

To protect class unity, avoid win/lose teacher-student and student-student confrontations. You force a teacher-student win/lose confrontation when you block a student without providing a detour.

- "Greg, I'm sorry, but you have to put the drawing away right now and turn to page 12 in your math book."
- "Alice, you have to participate. It's time to practice and we're all going to do our part in the choral reading."

Don't force the win/lose confrontation. Egos will get involved and it will easily become a battle of wills. Whenever this happens, you encourage an adversary relationship with your class.

PRINCIPLE: **Provide detours and alternatives.**

- "Greg, I know you want to finish your drawing, but I don't have time to explain math twice. You can either put that away now or find out how to do the math from another student."
- "Alice, you can either join the group now or see me after school to explain the situation."
- "Bill, the blocks are too noisy. Either work on a rug or put them away."
- "Girls, I can see we have a problem with the rules of the game. You can either try to work it out yourselves or go on to another activity. I'll be glad to discuss the problem with you at the end of recess."
- "Pete, you can either sit there in that chair or move it to a spot where you can still participate without interfering with others."

PRINCIPLE: **Avoid peer surveillance.**

One of the quickest ways to force student-to-student win/lose confrontations is to designate one student as the overseer of the rest. Having the class president list names of misbehaving students on the board or having a line monitor report who was goofing around will work, but there is a cost in terms of class unity. These techniques create friction between students, spawning problems on the playground as well as in the class. You not only create disturbances among students, but you also weaken class unity. The group becomes decentralized, forming small cliques, and peer pressure becomes less effective in shaping the behavior of the more difficult students. Consider alternatives to peer surveillance:

1. Have students learn to use "I Messages" with each other. (See page 195.)
2. Simply avoid or reduce the number of times and length of time students are left alone.
3. Have the class suggest alternative solutions.

PRINCIPLE: **Avoid trying to place blame; work instead on empathy and alternatives.**

One of the surest ways to force a student-to-student confrontation is to try to find out who started something or who was at fault.

Consider the following: One morning, Mrs. White's second grade enters the classroom, George picks up an eraser and hits Paul and Gilbert on their backs, leaving dust blotches on their coats. They turn around and start chasing George. George turns and runs into Betsy, knocking her down. She hits her head on a desk and starts to cry. This all happens in a matter of seconds. Mrs. White hurries over to Betsy to see that she's all right. She then turns around and tells George, Paul, and Gilbert to go to the office. Mrs. White turns her class over to her aide and follows the boys to the office. In the office, she asks the boys who started it. Paul and Gilbert put the blame on George. George denies it, saying he was just getting even for yesterday when they splashed mud on him after school.

When did it start? Don't pursue this question. This leads to a dead end. Finding fault doesn't help students learn to cope with similar situations. It will definitely lead to a win/lose situation where one student feels he hasn't been treated fairly.

Ask each child what happened, try to understand how they see the situation, label their feelings, acknowledge their concerns, and consider more acceptable ways of handling the situation. Don't try to find out who started it or point the finger of blame. Remember, what we consider as reality is only our perception of the situation. The important point is to try to help a student to see how the other student views the situation. *Don't invest your time in blame and shame; work instead on empathy and alternatives.*

Comments: Peer pressure can be a constructive force in terms of classroom management as long as you don't have an adversary relationship with your class. First, make your class appealing; then, work on developing and protecting class unity. Avoid such counterproductive moves as using peer surveillance and trying to place the blame on a student. These moves lead to win/lose confrontations which weaken class unity. Two other negative forces which should be avoided are the inappropriate use of competitive activities (see Chapter 8), and the inappropriate use of praise (see Chapter 12).

USING STUDENT INTERACTION TO BUILD CLASS UNITY

Once you have students wanting to cooperate, student interaction can be used to strengthen class unity. As students share their ideas, they learn more about each other and their respect for each other increases. Student participation will increase and with it there will be a greater feeling of responsibility and ownership of class activities. Class norms will be clarified, and this results in students realizing that there is general support for given policies and procedures and greater class unity.

PRINCIPLE: **Use class meetings to build group unity.**

One of the most effective ways to increase student interaction is through the use of class meetings. Several texts describing class meetings in detail are listed in the bibliography. The ideas that follow present techniques to use in leading class meetings.

ITEM 125. Pop-Up Discussions

This is a method that can be used initially in class meetings to help control discussions. As the teacher, you should start the discussion with a general question, or have the students raise an issue. Anyone who would like to respond to the question stands. All the rest of the students are seated. As soon as the first speaker finishes, anyone who would like to add something, pro or con, stands. If more than one is up, the speaker chooses one, the rest sit down, and the second speaker gives his views. After students learn a little control, this becomes a freely moving exchange of ideas.

Mrs. Phyllis Erickson
Northwood, Iowa

ITEM 126.   The Automatic Chairman

A tangible item (paper weight, football, anything to hold for turns) passes from person to person as the class sits in a circle. The person who is holding the item is automatically the chairman and is the only one who can talk. The item passes around the circle many times as the discussion progresses. As each student is given the item, he may or may *not* choose to contribute to the discussion.

Geraldine Hasley
Marion, Iowa

ITEM 127.   Generating Student Questions for Class Meetings

Once you have decided upon a subject area for discussion, distribute a 3″ x 5″ card to each student. Ask them to write *one* question-statement on the card. These should be anonymous. Collect the questions and place them in a covered coffee can or box.

Appoint a student moderator (as the teacher, you should join the circle, but let a student start the discussion). The moderator removes one question from the container and reads the question *twice*. The moderator waits a few seconds for reflection and then calls on a speaker to initiate the discussion. Your role is that of an active listener (rephrasing and clarifying student statements). After the students have finished reacting to the card, the moderator should ask, "Are you satisfied?" If satisfaction prevails, and time permits, another question should be selected.

Patricia L. Kay
Cedar Rapids, Iowa

ITEM 128.   Other Ways to Encourage Student Interaction

1. Redirect questions to several students before making a judgmental response: "Larry, do you agree with Scott?" "Mary, what do you think?"

2. Use silence (increase your wait-time after asking a question and after student responses).

3. Use an accepting strategy. When a student responds, avoid making a value judgment. Use such phrases as, "I understand," "Could be," and, "I see." Let the student know you hear the idea but don't pass judgment on it.

ITEM 129. Small Group Discussion Strategy

As with classroom meetings, the small group discussion strategy provides many opportunities for students to interact and compare ideas.

Divide your class into small groups of three or four students each. It is a good idea to keep the same groupings for several weeks or a month. A basic seating arrangement should be established so that the students can break up into groups without much teacher direction.

Possible uses of the small group strategy

1. "In five minutes, list as many words as you can that fit the slot found in the following sentence:

    "I was frightened by the _____ animal."

2. "List as many things as you can think of that might happen if a rich gold deposit was found in the Yosemite Valley."

3. "Reach an agreement on what Jan will do now that he knows he left his treasure box at Frau Wolff's farmhouse (reference to an episode in the book *Escape from Warsaw,* an excellent book to read orally to fifth and sixth graders)."

4. The small group discussion strategy is also effective for reinforcing a specific skill. Examples:

    a. "Using the system just demonstrated, make a list of all the possible rectangles found in the configuration displayed in Figure 7-1."

    b. "Classify the objects found in the bag under three headings. Each object must fit under one and only one heading."

    c. "Develop a good system to estimate how many kernels of rice are in the jar." Good is defined as accurate and quick.

5. You can also use the small group strategy to correct assignments.

    Example: "Check your answers on page 312. Reach an agreement about the correct answers. If your group decides on a different answer, feel free to change yours."

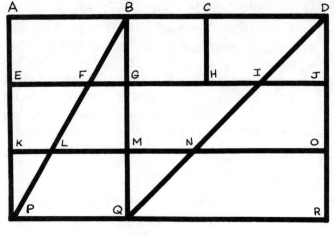

Figure 7-1

Specific techniques for using small group strategy

1. Provide a specific task. Write the focus question on the board so that the students can easily check to see if they are staying on task.

2. It is helpful to have students practice asking each other the following types of questions to encourage participation or clarify ideas: "George, what do you think about _____?" (A move to bring a nonparticipant into the discussion.) "George, are you saying that _____?" (A paraphrase or perception check to clarify what someone has said.)

Specific strengths of the small group strategy

1. This strategy allows for considerable active participation on the student's part.

2. It frees the teacher to become an observer, thus giving the teacher a chance to assess student progress.

3. This method stimulates divergent responses. Since the discussions are carried on simultaneously, many avenues are investigated rather than just one.

4. More students, especially the less aggressive, have the opportunity to enter the discussion and verbalize their feelings and ideas.

ITEM 130.   Quad Squads

At the beginning of the year, arrange the seating so that all students are working in groups of four. Assign the students to the groups at first, making certain that there is at least one good reader in each group. This helps take care of the nonreaders and lower level readers. These groups of four, or "quad squads," work through units as a total group and can serve as the basic unit for using the small group discussion strategy.

Mrs. Betty Parrish
Gainesville, Florida

ITEM 131.   Bit Problems

Bit problems are designed to encourage student participation and cooperation. The basic idea is that a group of students tries to solve a problem. Each student is given a clue or a set of clues. The students cannot show their clues to the other group members; however, they can read their clues or tell the other group members what information they have. The constraint of not being able to show the clues to the other students avoids the possibility that one student will collect all the clues and solve the problem while the others sit back and watch. In developing bit problems, you can simplify the task by varying:

1.   The number of participants in each group.
2.   The number of clues given to each member.
3.   The number and type of extraneous material included in the clues given to the students.
4.   The complexity of the problem.

Sample bit problems

1. *What does Gerald want?* (a five-bit problem) Directions: Divide your class into groups of five. Present the problem to the class (use the chalkboard or overhead projector). Give each student their set of clues. The strips in Figure 7-2 should be cut into three separate sets of clues. Remind them that they cannot show their clues to each other. Rather than involve the whole class, this activity would be best when used with one or two groups. In this way, the competitive aspect could be played down and skills of problem solving and cooperation could be emphasized.

Problem: What item does Gerald want and how much does it cost?

Clues: One slip for each student

Slip I
1.   The item is used for recreation.
2.   The item uses electricity.
3.   The first two letters of the item are ST.

Slip II
1.   The item can be used for solitary pleasure.
2.   The item price is in the hundreds of dollars.
3.   The digit in the one's place is a 9.

Slip III
1.   The digits after the decimal are the same. They are either 5's or 6's.
2.   You don't throw things at the item. It's not a dart board.
3.   The item plays something.

Slip IV
1.   The item ends with a long O sound, as in the word "bingo."
2.   Gerald's last name is Wright.
3.   The item can be enjoyed by a group.

Slip V
1.   The first digit in the price is a 2 (that is, the first digit reading from left to right).
2.   The digit in back of the 2 is a 3.
3.   There are no 5's in the price of the item.

Figure 7-2

2. *How many children are in our school?* Figure 7-3 presents a five-bit problem. This activity was designed for the primary level. A fishbowl technique could be used, placing five students in the center of the class, with the rest of the class sitting in a circle around the group. The students in the outer circle observe the group, noting how well they cooperate and use the information they are given. It is important to select students with loud voices for the inside group, to

Ideas to consider

The following concepts are listed to suggest possibilities. This list should never be used in one lesson.

1. All stores are in business to make a profit.
2. The sum of the digits for any multiple of 9 is 9.
3. All simple closed curves with a perimeter of 12 inches have the same area.
4. The product of the digits of any even number is always an even number.
5. Area is just another word for length times width.
6. A basketball doesn't have area.
7. North is always at the top of a map.
8. All children lose their teeth.
9. All cereals are good for you.
10. Getting angry is always bad.
11. The letter combination "ea" always has the long E sound as in "tea."
12. The word "the" is never capitalized in a title.

A series of concepts dealing with a highway map could also be used (see the sample worksheet in Figure 7-5).

Joyce Nelson
Cedar Rapids, Iowa

ITEM 133. Unique and Common

This is another activity designed to encourage active student involvement. It is an excellent language development activity and it provides an opportunity for discussing probability as it relates to decision making.

Have your students pair off or get into groups of three. Each group should have a recorder (scratch paper and pencil are needed). Tell the students they are to think of a unique word associated with anger, one they think none of the other groups will write down. Warn them that they must have the word written down by the time you give the signal. Count to five. Make sure you allow discussion time prior to your signal or countdown. If a group picks a word that is unique, they earn a point.

Concept Verification

Directions: Study your highway map carefully. Your group should agree on a rating for each statement. If the statement is true all of the time, and you can think of no exceptions, give it a 10. If the statement is never, or almost never true, give it a 1. Use the numbers between, that is 2, 3, 4, 5, 6, 7, 8, and 9, to indicate a rating between never true and always true.

Your group must decide on a rating. You may have to convince your group to decide on your rating. Do this by offering examples, making observations, or explaining the reasons for your choice. If someone in your group offers you proof, don't be afraid to change your mind. After studying the map, make the best decisions you can.

_____ 1. All large cities in Iowa are located on a river.

_____ 2. Highways colored in red or pink on the map are always wider than those drawn in black.

_____ 3. There are rest areas along all highways.

_____ 4. All highways run north-south or east-west.

_____ 5. All highways have only one name or one number.

_____ 6. All U.S. highways that run north-south are numbered with odd numbers.

_____ 7. The only way to cross the Mississippi River in a car is by bridge.

_____ 8. All towns are located on a road.

_____ 9. Most cities in Iowa have over 50,000 people.

_____ 10. Most small rivers flow from northwest to southeast.

Figure 7-5

In the case illustrated in Figure 7-6, Tom's and Jim's groups both picked "furious," so they don't get points, whereas the others picked unique words.

For the second part of round 1, the students write down a word they think everyone else will pick, the common word associated with anger. "Mad" was the common word, so Larry's, Tom's, Jim's, and Shannon's groups each earned a point.

In the second round of "Unique/Common," the students still use words associated with anger, but they can't use any words that were already listed.

Group Recorder	Round 1		Round 2		Round 3	
	Unique	Common	Unique	Common	Unique	Common
Tom	furious	mad				
Larry	angry	mad				
Sally	upset	furious				
Jim	furious	mad				
Roberto	boiling	furious				
Shannon	red	mad				

Figure 7-6

In this case, the activity has been presented as a competitive game with group scores being recorded. Larry's group has 2 points because they picked a unique word (angry) in the first part and the common word (mad) in the second part. You can change this into a cooperative game by recording the points in a common spot. In other words, the whole class would have received 4 points during the "unique phase" of round 1 and 4 points during the "common phase." The class could be challenged to see if they could get 20 points in three rounds. In this way, the students are pulling together and rooting for each other, rather than competing against one another.

The game can be played with a variety of content areas: planets, explorers, words associated with transportation, consonants, states, colors.

Comments: You can develop class unity by encouraging student interaction. Class meetings, the small group discussion strategy, the bit problems, and other activities presented in this section stimulate student discussion. This sharing of ideas helps students learn about each other, helps clarify class norms (peer group expectations), and helps correct faulty perceptions of what others think.

IMPORTANT CONSIDERATIONS IN DEVELOPING CLASSROOM RULES

One of the common ways teachers try to involve students and give them a feeling of ownership is in the development of class standards. This is a questionable practice. In most schools, behavior rules already exist either implicitly or explicitly. Asking students to help make these rules is a prime example of the "Answer Game." The suggestions are so predictable that the whole process is like a well rehearsed play.

Class Standards
We will respect our neighbor.
We will not run.
We will talk in a low voice.

The standards are not negotiable; the teacher and the students know what behavior is desired. The rules should merely be presented. The students can then help determine procedures or methods to use in trying to help each other follow them. The teacher should elicit student ideas regarding different plans with which to experiment. The emphasis is on scientific inquiry. "What can we do to keep the noise level down? ... No running is allowed in the halls, so what procedures should we follow in going to the library and cafeteria to help eliminate the running problem?" The students can suggest methods and help evaluate plans. In this case, all contributions can be considered and rationally dealt with. Asking students to formulate rules is merely going through the motions, merely "playing school." If you're interested in dignifying the student, make sure that the discussions and activities aren't rigged. Student contributions should matter and should be considered. There is room to experiment when it comes to implementing classroom rules. There is usually little tolerance in considering what the class rules are going to be.

ITEM 134. Enforcing Class Standards

The following steps are recommended as a procedure to help students follow class standards:

1. State the desired conduct for the given situation. Identify both appropriate and inappropriate behaviors.
2. Clarify the reason for the desired conduct.
3. Elicit student suggestions for ways to achieve the desired conduct and/or present various ideas of your own.
4. Have the students analyze the consequences of the various suggestions.
5. Get a commitment from the students to try a plan and decide on a system for evaluating its effectiveness.

6. Evaluate the plan at regular or daily intervals.

Comments: If the plan does not work, or if some students can't adhere to the plan, the problem is with the plan, not the children. Given the maturity levels of some or all of the students in the classroom, the plan is insufficient.

Often, you will have a problem spill over from recess into your classroom. Taking class time to discuss a problem related to kickball, four-square, or sharing the encyclopedia may seem like an ineffective use of class time. But the cumulative effect of this type of action may do much to clarify class norms.

It is easy to satisfy your conscience by having one or two lessons on something like values clarification and assume that you have covered your responsibility for the year. Your impact on a child's life does not come from one or two lessons, it comes from the way you treat that child day in and day out.

Taking the time to handle a concern should not be viewed as a nuisance but as an opportunity. When a concern is raised, give the class a chance to discuss the issue. Encourage student interaction, allow time to clarify norms, to sharpen thinking, and to develop new perceptions.

SUMMARY

Class unity can be a helpful or a destructive force. It all depends on whether you develop a supportive or adversary relationship with your class. If most of your students see your class as having appeal, if they want to cooperate, then peer pressure will work for you.

Hopefully, your program has appeal. If this is the case, then you want to maximize the benefits by building and protecting class unity. You protect class unity by avoiding win/lose situations, by avoiding the use of peer surveillance, and by avoiding the inappropriate use of competition and comparative praise.

You build class unity by building an enticing program and by encouraging student interaction. Students need an opportunity to learn how others feel in order to clarify class norms. Helping students share and discover mutual interests and concerns is one of the best ways to develop a sense of community and cooperation.

8

The Use and Abuse of Competitive and Cooperative Activities

1. Principles Related to the Use of Competition in the Classroom

    - Students should have an equal chance to win.

    - Students should have the chance to opt out.

    - As the teacher, if you compete with students, use a handicap instead of faking it.

    - Use the "everybody bats" strategy.

    - Competition is best suited for speed related tasks where simple recall is stressed.

    - Competition breaks class unity.

    - Success helps prepare children for the hardships of life. Consistent failure makes one vulnerable to emotional illness and less able to cope.

2. Changing Activities from a Competitive to a Cooperative Goal Structure

    - A competitive goal structure is best suited for low level, speed related learning objectives.

    - A cooperative goal structure is best suited for high level objectives where divergence of thought, problem solving skills, and empathy are desired outcomes.

PRINCIPLES RELATED TO THE USE OF COMPETITION IN THE CLASSROOM

ITEM 135. Competition is Only Motivating for Those Who Have a Chance to Win

The able are motivated by competition. They have a history of success and, in most situations, they have a good chance to win. For others, those who have the deck stacked against them, competition can be a frustrating experience which leads to inappropriate, nonresponsive, and obstructive behavior.

PRINCIPLE: **Students should have an equal chance to win.**

Whole class competitive activities are generally inappropriate because of the vast differences in ability found in most classes. Unless you are sure that the abilities are equally matched, students should be given the chance to opt out of any competitive event.

PRINCIPLE: **Students should have the chance to opt out.**

Students should be able to work at a small group or independent activity during a competitive event. If you force students into guaranteed loss situations, you're definitely weakening self-concepts. You're just proving again that the less able student is not capable and is a failure. It is criminal to force a student to stand in a spelling bee and listen to his peers complain:

- "Oh, no! What an easy word."
- "Anyone could have gotten that one right!"

Whether the comments are said in class, at recess, or just inferred from raised eyebrows or false smiles, the less able are still being subjected to abuse which is destructive to the self-concept. *Students should have the chance to opt out of competitive events.*

If students want to compete but are of unequal ability, other techniques can be used to help neutralize the difference. For example, you can add a chance factor. When the student gets a right answer, instead of getting a point, give the student a chance to roll a die or spin a dial. In this way, the student may pick up 1 to 6 points. To carry the idea another step, even if a student misses the question, he could still get a chance to roll a die. The dice could be altered so that one has the normal sides (1, 2, 3, 4, 5, and 6) while another has new values assigned (1, 5, 6, 4, 5, and 6). The student who misses rolls the first die with less chance for high points. The winner rolls the altered die and will probably roll a higher score. Rolling dice has an added benefit. The added excitement of rolling dice, spinning a dial, or picking a number out of a hat changes the focus from one's success or failure in answering a question to the excitement of chance. For the loser, this really helps protect the self-concept. It's similar to the technique of having a student who has just missed a problem at the board call on someone to come up and help. In this case, the student's failure of missing a problem is soon forgotten because he now has a reward to pass out.

Another technique that can be used is the handicap system. For example, if one student is more skilled at checkers than another, they may only get to start the game with six pieces. In chess, if one student is more skilled than another, he may start without a queen or the bishops. Or, in a game situation, one student may only get one turn while the other gets three or can continue as long as he is successful. The basic idea is to think of some creative way to handicap students to compensate for differences in ability.

PRINCIPLE: **As the teacher, if you compete with students, use a handicap instead of faking it.**

If you're competing with students, don't fake it so the students will win. Having an opponent play easy is demoralizing and a victory so won has a bitter taste. Students know their abilities. They are quick to spot a phony. If you want to dignify the student, you shouldn't "let him win." A better strategy is to either spot the student some points or handicap yourself as described above.

PRINCIPLE: Use the "everybody bats" strategy.

The "everybody bats" principle means that, in a game like baseball or kickball, everyone on a side gets to bat each inning, instead of only being up until three outs are made.

It is threatening for the poor player, the slow maturer, and the uncoordinated to come to bat when your team has two outs. You take a lot of pressure off the situation if you give everyone a chance to bat during each inning.

PRINCIPLE: Competition is best suited for speed related tasks where simple recall is stressed.

In a competitive activity, students or teams of students are working against each other. In a class situation, this is counterproductive if you're trying to promote high level thinking. Competition is best suited for low level tasks (recognition and recall) such as memorizing arithmetic facts, spelling words, abbreviations, or state capitals.

If you look at some of the high level thinking skills (predicting, making inferences, evaluating, empathizing), you want students to share ideas and to build upon each other's thinking. A competitive atmosphere is not conducive to this type of thinking.

ITEM 136. Don't Use Competition to Manage Your Class

PRINCIPLE: Competition breaks class unity.

Many teachers rely too heavily on competition in managing their classrooms. When you excuse kids by the quietest row, the neatest desks, or the best papers, you are pitting student against student. You are guaranteeing a win/lose situation. Every class has a Sloppy Sam or a Wild Willy. A student sitting in Wild Willy's row hasn't got a chance to be the first one excused so that he can get the best diamond at recess. By using the "best row" technique, you accentuate the misery of some students by turning them against each other.

Instead of having students compete against each other, have them compete against a standard.

- "If all but three of you are cleaned up by 3:15, we'll start dismissing."
- "On the spelling test, if at least 18 of you miss less than two, you'll all get an extra 10 minutes added to your free-choice time."

You don't want your students coming down hard on Terrible Tom or Sloppy Sam. You want them to help each other and be supportive. Setting cooperative goals helps insure unity, whereas competition can be destructive.

The same principle holds true when applied at the level of the whole school. In making your class more appealing to students, don't compete with other faculty members. Don't try to increase your status at the expense of another teacher. Work cooperatively, share ideas, and invite others to try your new activities.

PRINCIPLE: **Success helps prepare children for the hardships of life. Consistent failure makes one vulnerable to emotional illness and less able to cope.**

We learn about ourselves as we are mirrored in the eyes of others. When students are placed in failure situations, when they are subject to scorn and ridicule by their peers, they get confirmation that they are not able and not well liked. This is a destructive rather than humbling process.

Realizing that someone is more capable than you can be a good experience because it is humbling, but being constantly confronted with a situation where you know you're going to lose is a destructive experience. Much of the competition used in schools is of the destructive variety.

Comments: In many classrooms, competition is used inappropriately. Frequently, activities are organized on a whole class basis and many times students of unequal ability are forced to compete against each other. Competition is used in lessons with high level objectives where cooperative learning should be stressed. Furthermore, students are seldom given the chance to opt out of a competitive activity, thus forcing the anxious and less able into public demonstrations of their ignorance and lack of skill. These poor practices are destructive to self-concepts, to class unity, and to teaching effectiveness.

CHANGING ACTIVITIES FROM A COMPETITIVE TO A COOPERATIVE GOAL STRUCTURE

Definitions

Competitive goal structure. This is a win/lose situation where students or groups of students compete against each other. Differences in ability present a problem as students do not react favorably unless they think they have an equal chance to win.

PRINCIPLE: **A competitive goal structure is best suited for low level, speed related learning objectives.**

Cooperative goal structure. With a cooperative goal structure, students are trying to accomplish a common goal. Rather than competing with each other, students try to share their knowledge and skills to help achieve a common goal. Variations in ability are valued and do not present the same threat that is present in competitive situations.

PRINCIPLE: **A cooperative goal structure is best suited for high level objectives where divergence of thought, problem solving skills, and empathy are desired outcomes.**

ITEM 137. The Clap Game

The class forms a circle. The teacher starts a clapping rhythm (clap, clap, rest). Once the rhythm is established, the teacher names a category (trees) on a rest. On the next rest (clap, clap, *rest*), the student standing on the teacher's right must name an item that fits the category (see Figure 8-1). On the next rest (clap, clap, *rest*), the next student to the right must name another item that fits the category. The items can't be duplicated and the rhythm must be maintained. If a student can't think of another item or if the student doesn't say it on the next rest, he is out. The game continues until all but one have been eliminated.

When a student misses, the student is out and the teacher moves into that spot (Teacher 2). The teacher then names a new category and the game continues.

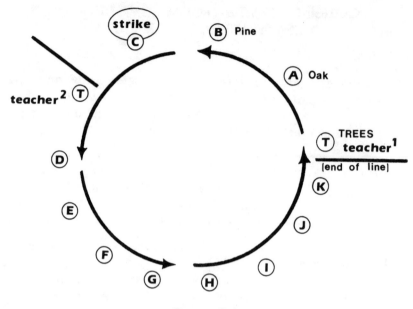

Figure 8-1

As described, this activity uses a competitive goal structure. The educational objective is to review items included in different categories (explorers, states west of the Mississippi, planets, birds, etc.). This is a rather low level skill in which students do not have to empathize, draw inferences, or make predictions. Because the activity has a low level objective, a competitive goal structure is appropriate.

The next question to examine is whether the students in the group have an equal chance to win. If not, you have the problem always present with competitive activities: the weak get eliminated and the strong remain. The ones who don't need it get more practice and experience. This problem can be partially eliminated if you have the student who misses go to the end of the line rather than being eliminated. In this way, the student who misses will get a second turn before the successful students get a second chance. If you're going to use the process of elimination, instead of going all the way down until one student is left, you might call the game when ten students are left. These ten are declared winners and the game starts again. After the game has been modeled several times, small groups may be formed and they may play the game separately. In this case, the last student to name an item successfully gets to name the new category. If you let the students select their own groups, the ones with like abilities will usually gravitate toward each other.

Even though a competitive goal structure is appropriate for this objective, consider the benefits of changing the Clap Game into one using a cooperative goal structure. You could easily change it into a cooperative activity by counting each miss as a pass (no point). In this way, you could see how many points or unique items could be named as you go once around the circle. In the example depicted in Figure 8-2, the class scored 8 points.

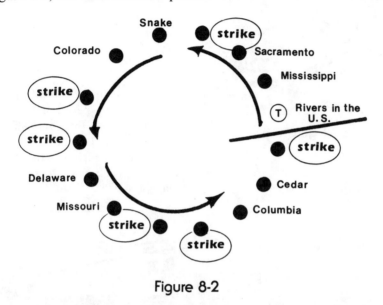

Figure 8-2

As a cooperative activity, you might first start with a brainstorming session, with students trying to name as many items as they can for the given category. Students could also talk about ways to be prepared with two items so that if the person in front of one student names that student's item, he will still have one left. Other problems could be listed and possible solutions generated. Here we have a cooperative, supportive atmosphere. There will certainly be a payoff from this approach in terms of growth for the less able student and in terms of class unity.

ITEM 138. Matched Pairs

Appropriately sized pictures are glued onto 3″ × 5″ cards (see Figure 8-3). Approximately 30 cards will be needed. Cut each card in half. You should end up with 60 cards, each having half of a picture.

A student is called to the front of the class to describe one of his half-cards (see Figure 8-4).

Figure 8-3

"I have the left side of a park. It looks like a pencil or charcoal drawing. I have the front half of a bus or van. The bus is in the middle of my picture. You should have the back half. Does anyone have a match?"

Figure 8-4

The rest of the students listen to the description and check their cards. If they think they have a match, they raise their hands. The student up front calls on a student who has raised his hand. They check for a match. If it is, the student who described the card places the match on his desk and both students draw a replacement card from the desk. The student who was called on (whether a successful match was made or not) gets to describe the next card. The student with the most matches is the winner.

The game could be changed into a cooperative activity by using one of the following strategies:

1. See if the class can get five matches before recess.

2. See if you can beat your record of ten matches in 5 minutes.

3. Have the students ask questions before they check to see if they have a match:
   "Does the bus have snow on its top?"
   "Is the bus in the middle part of the picture?"
   "Is the sky dark?"

With this strategy, an attempt would be made to avoid any mismatches. ("See if you can limit yourself to three mismatches while making ten matches.")

If you played this as a competitive game (seeing who could get the most matches), you would have one winner and a whole class of losers. With a cooperative activity, you have a much healthier situation.

ITEM 139. Space Tower

The class is divided into groups of three to five. The game proceeds as follows:

1. Tell the class that each group is going to be given a 5-minute time period to plan how to build a tall structure out of computer cards. The completed structure must be able to support a tennis ball. Explain that each group will be given a stack of computer cards, two pairs of scissors, and a tennis ball.

2. Once the 5-minute planning period expires, each group will have 20 minutes to complete their structure. Stress that once the 20-minute work period starts, no talking will be allowed.

3. Pass out the materials and start the 5-minute planning period.

4. After 5 minutes pass, review the assignment and start the work period. After 20 minutes, call time. Have the students measure their towers and test them to see if they'll

support a tennis ball. The group with the tallest tower that supports a tennis ball is declared a winner.

This is a problem solving activity and, as such, a cooperative goal structure would be more appropriate than a competitive structure. Rather than challenge the students to see who can build the tallest structure, each group could be given a unique challenge such as:

1. See if you can build a structure that is over 18 inches tall and will support a tennis ball.

2. Build a structure that will support two tennis balls, both of which are equidistant from the table or base.

3. Build a structure that is wider at the top than at the bottom and will still support a tennis ball.

4. Build a structure, having a height three times the width of its base, that will support a tennis ball.

A series of challenges like this will cut down on the competitive nature of the activity and encourage a cooperative problem solving approach. You could provide each group with a planning period, calling the groups together, having them share their ideas, and then give each group 20 minutes in which to work. Talking could be allowed during the work period. The constraint of no talking provides practice in detailed planning and may not be appropriate in this case.

A picture of each completed project could be taken, and these could be added to a bulletin board, in the office or classroom, entitled, "Working Together Can Produce..."

Adapted from an idea submitted by:
Jill Wagner
Iowa City, Iowa

ITEM 140.   Vowel Dominoes

Purpose of game:

1. To reinforce auditory discrimination between short and long vowels.

2. To reinforce sound-symbol association of the patterns for short or long vowel sounds.

Game equipment:

One set of 60 dominoes showing pictures with names containing short or long vowel sounds.

Basic game directions:

1. Two to six players may play the game.

2. All dominoes are placed face down in center of table.

3. Players draw in turn until each has five dominoes.

4. The first player to draw a double domino begins the play. The double is placed face up in the center of the table.

5. The second player adds a domino with a matching sound to the side of the first double domino. He announces the sound and words he is matching. Single dominoes are matched end to end with other single dominoes, and end to side with double dominoes, as in the regular domino game.

6. The object of the game is to be the first person to run out of dominoes. If you cannot play from your five dominoes, you draw from the reserve. If no one has used all of their dominoes before the reserve is gone, the person with the fewest dominoes is the winner.

Again, this is organized as a competitive activity. Given the objective, a competitive goal structure would be appropriate as long as the students were of equal ability. Changing the game to a cooperative goal structure alleviates the problem of one child winning and also takes away the threat of losing.

You could have each player choose two characters to represent a winner and a non-winner. Favorite ones include Snoopy characters, professional sports teams, and TV stars. Before the game begins, the students decide who they want as their point makers and who will be the villains (non-winners). Given the time you have, estimate how many points you think the student can reasonably make. You might challenge the group by saying, "If Snoopy gets at least 25 points in the 15 minutes that we have, you will all receive a scratch-and-smell strawberry sticker."

In modifying the game, each player keeps five dominoes in front of him at all times until the reserve is gone. This eliminates the first person who runs out of dominoes from becoming a winner. If the student plays correctly, the character designated as the winner gets the point. If a student mismatches vowel sounds or fails to recognize a play, the villain gets the point. It is a cooperative battle to collect enough points for the reward and all children benefit from the practice that the game provides.

Roberta Swanson
Iowa City, Iowa

ITEM 141. Dismissing Children

A competitive goal structure is often used to dismiss students: "The island of children that gets quiet fastest may go first to wash hands, put on coats, and line up with their lunch tickets at the door."

This could be changed into a cooperative goal structure by using one of the ideas listed below, coupled with the following systematic way of dismissing students. A simple schedule is posted where everyone can see that Monday's group is Lila's Island, Tuesday's is Amy's, and so on. Each island knows which day they are to be dismissed first, and that it has nothing to do with who is quietest, but is just part of the regular routine.

- "I'm going to turn my back and close my eyes. When the whole class is ready to go, Jason may come and tap me on the back."

- "As soon as 80 percent of you are ready to go, we'll start dismissing."

- "We'll start dismissing at 11:23, so please see that you are ready."

Kathy Kron
Iowa City, Iowa

ITEM 142. Multiplication Bridge

Purpose: To give added experience in multiplying by 10, 100, 1000, and 10,000.

Materials: Old decks of cards (bridge). One with missing cards may be used.

Procedure: Separate the cards into two stacks, one pile Ace through 9, the second pile 10 through King. Divide the first pile into two stacks, leaving you with three stacks of cards. The three stacks are then placed face down. Give a value to the face cards, such as 10 equals 10, Jack equals 100, Queen equals 1000, and King equals 10,000. A student can then draw one card from each pile, or three different students may draw from the piles. Cards drawn might be 9, 3, and Jack which would be $9 \times 3 \times 100$. The people who draw the cards may work the problems at the board while the rest of the class work at their desks. It may be solved in many ways $(9 \times 3) \times 100 = 2700$; $9 \times (3 \times 100) = 2700$; $100 \times (9 \times 3) = 2700$. The face cards may be given other values and the game can be modified to review addition processes as well.

As a competitive activity, the team to write the correct answer on the board first is the winner (each group has a designated writer).

As a cooperative activity, a time limit could be established. The class gets a point for each student who successfully computes and writes the answer in the allotted time. Students could share the methods they use and hints for saving time to help other students who are having difficulty.

Helen Daume
Anita, Iowa

ITEM 143. Football Facts

Purpose: To give practice in multiplication facts.

Materials: Cut ten footballs from ten sheets of brown construction paper or oaktag. Make ten footballs that are large and easy to handle. On each football, place a number, 0 through 9 (see Example A in Figure 8-5). On ten sheets of oaktag or cardboard 12" × 9", place numbers 0 through 9 (see Example B in Figure 8-5).

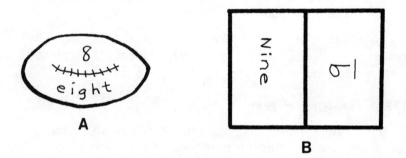

Figure 8-5

Procedure: Divide the class into two teams. Lay the rectangular cards in a line on the floor, mixed up, a footstep apart. Place the numbered footballs upside down on the table. The team going first will have their first player pick a football. The student then starts at one end of the line (floor) carrying his football and states the whole fact with the answer. If he can go the entire line of ten cards with the ball, stating correct answers, 7 points is given to the team. The football is returned to the pile of footballs, mixed in, and the other team sends their first player to draw a ball and go the line. In the event that an error is made (a fumble), the opposing team may take the ball for the remainder of the line. If that player gives a correct answer and the rest of the line correctly answered, they get the points. Alternate players each time.

Helen Daume
Anita, Iowa

As a cooperative activity, the game could be adapted so that the class represents a team. Each time a player goes to the line, he earns 7 points for the team; however, if he fumbles and misses an item, the player must draw a situation card which might read:

1. Your opponents intercepted and ran back for a touchdown. They get 7 points.
2. The opposing team has gone on a rampage and scored 28 points.
3. The opposing team tipped the ball right into the hands of one of your teammates. Pick someone and let them continue down the line.
4. You ran backwards and you were tackled in the end zone. The other team gets 2 points for a safety.

A whole series of cards could be made to add humor, to give the other team a chance to win, and to let the student who fumbled have a chance to redeem himself.

ITEM 144. Mystery Erase

Take any list of words (original 13 colonies, abbreviations for six states, names of students in the room) and display them on the overhead projector or the chalkboard. Ask the students to put their heads down. Cover one of the words or erase it and call for heads up. The students have to raise their hands and name the word that was erased (possibly spell it, locate it on a map, or point to the correct child). Expose the word and check to see if the student was right. Cover the word again and call for heads down. Cover a second word. Call heads up and ask the student to name the two missing words, in the order in which you covered them. Continue covering more words until the students are stumped.

As a competitive activity, you could pit team against team. When a team cannot name the items in the order in which they were covered, they are eliminated. The winning team for each round earns a point.

As a cooperative activity, students could be challenged to see how many items they can remember before they get stumped. They could be given time to devise plans to help remember the progression in which the items were covered and for figuring out which new item was covered.

ITEM 145. Oh My Word

"Oh My Word" was adapted from a TV program of the same name. In this case, three panel members are needed. The panel members are given a card similar to those shown in Figure 8-6.

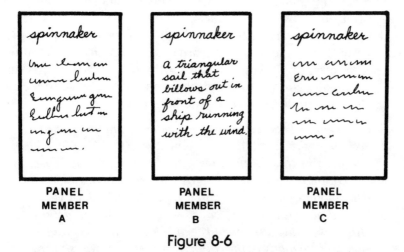

PANEL	PANEL	PANEL
MEMBER	MEMBER	MEMBER
A	B	C

Figure 8-6

After the teacher gives each panel member a card, he presents the word to the class. In presenting the word, the pronunciation is usually reviewed as well as different phonetic principles related to the word. ("If the word was spelled 'spinaker,' how would it be pronounced?") While the teacher is doing this, the three panel members are thinking of a definition for their word. One panel member is given the correct definition and doesn't have to make up a definition.

After the teacher has presented the word, each panel member is called upon to give a definition. The other students listen to the definitions and try to determine which one is correct. In this case, the panel members might say:

A. "A spinnaker is a type of irrigation device similar to a rainbird."

B. "A spinnaker is a sail on a ship. It is found in the front part of the ship."

C. "A spinnaker is an ancient type of Chinese fireworks that rotates wildly as it burns."

The students are divided into teams of three to five students. After the three definitions are given, they discuss among themselves which is the correct definition. At a signal, they hold up a 3" × 5" card to signify whether their group has selected A, B, or C. The correct definition is then given and points are allotted accordingly. To make this a cooperative activity, you can have the class as a whole try to beat the panel. Each correct choice earns a point for the class, and you subtract a point for each incorrect choice.

When the game is introduced, the students should be given suggestions on how to make their definitions believable: (1) try to make your definitions fairly detailed, (2) try to use difficult words in your definition, (3) look at your card as you're giving the definition so that the class thinks you're using information from the cards, and (4) occasionally go over to the teacher and ask what a word means, even though you don't have any definition given on your card.

Comments: This section has presented eight competitive activities with suggestions on how to change them from a competitive to a cooperative goal structure. In each case, the cooperative version avoids the problems associated with having one winner and a number of losers. At the same time, student problem solving, student interaction, and class unity are encouraged. One of the techniques suggested in many of the cooperative versions was sharing of ideas among students. There is a real payoff in this strategy in terms of being able to dignify students and their contributions.

SUMMARY

Competition motivates those who have a good chance to win but it can also be destructive to self-concepts and fuel an uncooperative, get-the-other-guy atmosphere that can be detrimental to your success as a classroom manager.

A competitive goal structure is best suited for low level recall, recognition, and drill-type activities. When competition is used appropriately, students should be of equal ability and should be able to opt out of the competitive activity.

Many of the competitive activities currently used can be modified into a cooperative goal structure. This is recommended, because it will help develop class unity, increase positive self-concepts, and reduce class conflicts.

9

Being Consistent While
Recognizing Student Differences

1. When Should You Be Consistent?
   - Most disciplinary situations call for teaching, not punishment.
   - Fixed responses should only be used for serious offenses or when the student is openly defying established policy.
2. Recognizing and Dealing with Different Levels of Moral Reasoning
   - Learning takes place on a continuum.
   - Kohlberg's Levels of Moral Decision Making.
3. Helping Students Accept Differential Treatment
   - Don't limit your teaching to whole class activities.
   - Differential treatment helps a student prepare for life's inequities.
   - It is difficult to change one's position once it is stated publicly.

WHEN SHOULD YOU BE CONSISTENT?

"There is nothing so unequal as the equal treatment of unequals."—Brandywine

"Don't be consistent." Heresy, you say? No, just good advice.

If you look at the cause of most misbehavior in the elementary classroom, you'll usually find that poor judgment, not open defiance, is the culprit. This is an important distinction.

If a problem has resulted from poor judgment, then your reaction should be to teach, and to try to change student perceptions.

PRINCIPLE: **Most disciplinary situations call for teaching, not punishment.**

When you have students fighting over a chair, running in the room, playing at the sink, or tripping other students in the aisle, you are generally dealing with ego-centered, fun-loving myopia. You're not dealing with evil thoughts, open defiance, or personal attacks against you and your system. You're dealing with poor judgment, not sinful acts of disobedience.

This being the case, you should react with teaching, not punishment. The good teacher recognizes individual differences and acts accordingly. Differential treatment should be used in reacting to most misbehavior. Students have different abilities, operate at different levels of moral reasoning, and circumstances will vary; thus, your reactions should vary.

170

PRINCIPLE: **Fixed responses should only be used for serious offenses or when the student is openly defying established policy.**

Consistency becomes important when you administer punishment as a deterrent or natural consequence of an act (see Chapter 11). Whenever you punish, you run the risk of being perceived as unfair. Some will see you as too harsh, others as too easy. If you're inconsistent in how you administer punishment to different children, you increase the likelihood of appearing unfair.

So, in terms of meting out punishments, you should be consistent, but the use of punishment should not be a mainline defense. It should be reserved for serious offenses; thus, most of your reactions should be characterized by differential treatment and not by consistent, fixed responses. The question of what is a serious offense becomes important here. The definitions established by the Hillsborough Public Schools may be helpful:

> *Serious offenses are those which, if done off school grounds, are likely to draw attention of other authorities such as police. Examples of serious offenses include: alcohol, assault, drugs, possession of weapons, theft or extortion, and vandalism. Examples of "objective" offenses include: alcohol, assault, drugs, fighting, possession of weapons, smoking violations, tardiness, trespassing, truancy, and vandalism. Using this breakdown, the subjective offenses become: disobedience, disruptive or disrespectful behavior, obscenity or profanity, threats, and the like.*

(Source: *Discipline Practices in the Hillsborough County Public Schools,* a study by the Florida School Desegregation Consulting Center, the University of Miami, Coral Gables, Florida, Dr. Gordon Foster, Director, April 1, 1977.)

If your school does not have established guidelines for reacting to the more serious offenses, you may want to encourage their development. A good set of guidelines has been prepared by the Pennsylvania Department of Education Commissioner's Task Force on Student Responsibility and Discipline:

The task force acknowledges the need for teachers and administrators to exercise discretion in dealing with student misconduct. A rigid system of mandatory discipline responses for certain offenses seldom proves workable because it fails to recognize the specific circumstances surrounding some instances of misconduct. On the other hand, discipline administered by a case-by-case basis with considerable flexibility of response is often inconsistent, inappropriate and inequitable.

In consideration of the limitations inherent in either of these approaches to discipline, the task force makes the following recommendations:

1. *Conduct and discipline codes should explicitly define unacceptable student behavior and should carefully describe the disciplinary actions attached to each incident of misconduct. Where several options might be appropriate for the same type of offense, the circumstances under which each would be applied should be noted.*
2. *Fixed responses should be prescribed for certain offenses. The more serious kinds of misconduct generally should elicit the same type of action in each instance. Discretion in administering the recommended punishment should be applied only in unusual circumstances.*
3. *Every effort should be made to avoid situations which imply preferential treatment in the administration of discipline. Policies and practices should apply equally to all students.*
4. *All school staff members should know the student conduct and discipline code and should use it consistently in all cases of student misconduct. Violations of the code should never be ignored, and all offenders should be dealt with in a manner consistent with the code.*

It should be stated again that at the elementary level, most problems, although bothersome, are going to be relatively minor and punishment should not be used.

Comments: Most problem situations at the elementary level result from poor judgment. Students don't consider the possible consequences of an act. They are more concerned about getting someone's attention than they are about following the day's lesson. They want to have fun by playing a trick on someone or performing some other mischief. These are matters of perceptions and value conflicts. Your response should vary with the situation. You should teach, not punish.

Your responses to minor infractions will vary. Sometimes you will ask a student to see you at recess and other times you may merely remind a child of what is expected. You are consistent in the sense that you have a basic rationale for why you respond the way you do, but you do not consistently dish out fixed punishments. This would be poor teaching because it does not recognize individual differences and treats the students as wards or inmates needing constant surveillance and guarding. Having fixed responses to all infractions will maintain order, but it avoids your central obligation of helping children to mature.

Consider the following cases:

1. *The book drop.* At 10:14, all the books in your math class hit the floor (see Figure 9-1). You're working on papers at your desk. What do you do?

Your response should be controlled by your perception of why the students pulled the "drop." Are they out to get you? Are they inquisitive about how you'll react? Are they merely having some fun?

If you react with punishment, especially a set punishment (participation in a book drop equals 30 minutes after school), you're in for a rocky trip. Your immediate reaction could be one of many (see Chapter 10):

- Humor
- Compliment their ingenuity
- A nonverbal sign (smiling, shaking of head, rolling eyes)
- "I message"

Reaction with a set punishment would only be in line if this was one of many "drops" and time had been spent discussing the why's

Figure 9-1

and why not's of book drops. Given this history, participation in a book drop could be construed as an open act of defiance; otherwise, you should react by teaching, not by punishing.

2. *The old penny in the faucet trick.* One of your clever charges may try to set you up by jamming a penny in the end of a faucet (see Figure 9-2). The word is passed around class and no one takes a drink. They wait, gleefully anticipating your shock.

Figure 9-2

Do you react with punishment or do you acknowledge the clever stunt and try to help your students understand why you don't appreciate teaching class and walking around school with water marks on your pants? The second time may be a different story, but initially you should not react with any set punishment.

3. *The potato gun.* A student is caught shooting bits of potato across the room. See the potato gun pictured in Figure 9-3. Don't react with 50 sentences or assign detention. Consider the student's motivation. You'll be much more effective in the long run if you don't react with a set punishment. Acknowledge the student's motivation and try to help the student to see why such playfulness cannot be permitted.

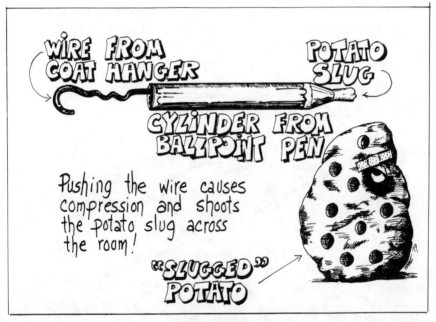

Figure 9-3

The student knows he shouldn't be playing with the potato gun, but the fun and temptation is too overpowering. It's a matter of maturity and goals. Deal with these by recognizing the conflict in goals and by trying to change perceptions. Don't immediately react in a punitive manner.

In terms of consistency, your comments with one child may be more direct and threatening than with another, but this reflects factors such as past history and the timing of the incident. It must, if you are going to teach effectively. If your standard reaction is punishment, then consistency is important and so is malpractice insurance.

RECOGNIZING AND DEALING WITH DIFFERENT LEVELS OF MORAL REASONING

PRINCIPLE: **Learning takes place on a continuum.**

Decisions made by students, their behavior, their perceptions of your behavior, and their whole sense of justice reflect their level of maturity.

As depicted in Figure 9-4, researchers have shown that we go through levels of moral development as we mature. This knowledge is very important as we address the whole issue of reacting to misbehavior.

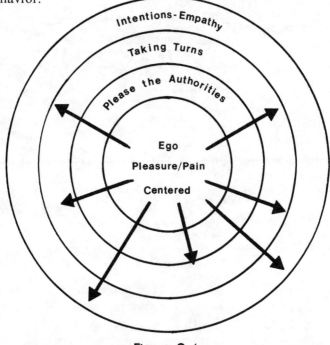

Figure 9-4

Kohlberg's Stages of Moral Reasoning

Since the 1950s, Lawrence Kohlberg, his colleagues, and many other researchers have conducted descriptive research which

- Try to consider how a change in a given situation might affect one's view.
- Label feelings.
- Identify value conflicts.
- Suggest value sources.
- List possible consequences of different value positions.

4. *Use a nonjudgmental teaching strategy.* When you're discussing an issue, try to promote student debate. Students will grow from exposure to other views, from verbalizing their ideas, and from confronting conflicting ideas.

Redirect questions. Redirect questions to avoid premature closure and to encourage student interaction. Ask several students the same question before you respond: "Phil, that's one idea. Jane, what do you think? Pete? Carl?" In this way, debate is encouraged and more students become actively involved.

Probe for clarification. In using an accepting strategy, it is important to probe for clarification. To accept a student's answer without understanding demonstrates a certain degree of insincerity. Probe the child for clarification: "Help me understand what you are saying here, I don't understand what you mean by ..."

Avoid closure. Avoid simplistic solutions. Ask students to consider alternatives and related contingencies: "What would you think if six of you were involved, instead of two?" "Would that be the best solution if Jim was a stranger instead of a classmate?"

Don't pass judgment. You will encourage student participation by avoiding judgmental responses. For example, use such phrases as: "That's one idea," "I understand," "Your idea is... Does someone have another idea?"

5. *Vary your feedback according to the developmental level of the students.* When you're reacting to your students' ability to follow class standards and carry out directives, vary your feedback according to their developmental level.

Primary aged children should be reinforced for their obedience but, for older children, the stress should be placed on goal achievement, on the products of cooperative behavior.

Comments such as , "I like the way you ... ," place the emphasis on pleasing the teacher, pleasing the authority in charge. This is appropriate for students who are operating on level 1, but it should not be the standard fare because it models level 1 thought. Stress the reasons why you're pleased, not just the fact that you're pleased.

Comments: One of the reasons teachers should not consistently react with fixed punishments to misbehavior is that the misbehavior more than likely represents poor judgment on the student's part. This presents an excellent vehicle for teachers to model a higher level of moral decision making. Most primary students will have a punishment/obedience orientation (Kohlberg's level 1); therefore, the teacher should emphasize sharing and taking turns (level 2) and also place some stress on a person's intentions and on trying to understand the other's point of view (level 3). Level 1 statements will do little to help the students in the long run. Examine the response patterns displayed in Figures 9-5 and 9-6.

Level 1 (Pleasure/Pain) (Please the Authority)	Level 2 (Reciprocity)	Level 3 (Intentions/Peer Pressure) (Good Boy/Empathy)
Student Behavior: Michael talks out of turn.		
"Michael, I told you to take turns."	"Michael, it's Cheryl's turn now. You'll have a chance in a minute."	"Michael, I know you have something you want to share, but remember our class rules?"
Student Behavior: Susan and Jim fight over a ball.		
"If you can't play with that ball without fighting, I'll take it away."	"Susan, why don't you use it this recess and Jim can have it after lunch?"	"Jim and Sue, I know you both want the ball. Let's see if we can work out a game with the rest of the students."
Student Behavior: Rachel calls Roberta a name.		
"Rachel, if there's any more name-calling, you'll have to go back to your seat."	"Rachel, how would you like it if everyone called you names?"	"Rachel, even though you don't mean to hurt Roberta, your name-calling is really bothering her. Do you remember when we talked about teasing and how some of the others felt?"

Figure 9-5

With intermediate students, teacher responses should basically fall into Level 2 and 3, with some stress on Level 4.

Level 2 (Reciprocity)	Level 3 (Intentions/Peer Pressure) (Good Boy /Empathy)	Level 4 (Law and Order)

Student behavior: Bud puts his lips to the faucet when he takes a drink.

"Bud, I don't want your germs any more than you want mine."	"Bud, how do you think the others feel when they see your mouth on the faucet like that?"	"Bud, remember the standard the class agreed to? Don't touch the spout when you're drinking."

Student behavior: Ann is peeking during a game.

"Ann, it's not fair to the others if you see and they don't."	"Ann, I know you're just excited. Remember, no peeking."	"Ann, we can't have a game without playing by the rules. The game will fall apart if we don't follow the rules."

Student behavior: Cindy is cheating on a spelling test.

"Cindy, if you write the hard words on your wrist like that, it's not fair to the others who have studied hard."	"Cindy, I know getting 100 percent is important to you, but think how the others would feel if they knew you were cheating."	"Cindy, we should all do our best and strive for good grades. But, if we want to feel good about our accomplishments, we'd better play by the rules."

Figure 9-6

Comments: Telling a second grade student that "when you cheat you only hurt yourself," is ineffective. Such a comment is too abstract for a child operating on level 1, 2, or 3. Ask a seven-year-old to paraphrase that comment and see if he rephrases it using level 2 or level 3 reasoning. Remember: Most students will not be able to comprehend reasoning more than one level above their current thinking. Remember also that modeling thinking which is at or below a student's current level does little to raise his level of moral decision making.

Avoid fixed responses to problem situations because this does not help students mature in their reasoning. If you consistently react with the same punitive measures to control misbehavior, you are responding with level 1 thinking and stunting your students' growth. Your reactions should vary and should not operate on a pleasure/pain principle.

HELPING STUDENTS ACCEPT DIFFERENTIAL TREATMENT

Differential treatment should be used in assignments, in selecting teaching strategies, and in the way you react to off-task behavior.

PRINCIPLE: **Don't limit your teaching to whole class activities.**

Some teachers pass over exciting learning activities because they don't see how the whole class can be involved or because the activity would be too expensive if everyone did it. This includes activities such as using a microscope, making a leather belt, preparing a slide program, or making taffy.

In the same vein, some teachers avoid using behavior modification plans with desirable and/or expensive contingencies (free pass to a baseball game, five free plays on a pinball machine, lunch with the principal), because it would be too expensive if everyone did it and, if only a few got the chance, the others would complain.

The fact is, students will feel it's unfair and they will complain. This is natural and should be expected, but it does not mean that differential treatment should be avoided.

PRINCIPLE: **Differential treatment helps a student prepare for life's inequities.**

The use of differential treatment respects individual differences and helps students learn to cope with life. Most teachers have successfully handled the use of differential assignments. Reading groups have different assignments, students read different materials, groups differ in size. Students seem to accept differences in reading ability as teachers do. But, when it comes to differences in how a teacher reacts to misbehavior, this is another story.

Students can see that one student reads better than another. They can see differences in ability. Differences in social behavior are also visible, but seldom are students grouped by their ability to sit quietly or by their moral reasoning ability, nor have expectations been established that such distinctions should be made.

Young children will have a problem accepting differential treatment. In fact, very young children may not be able to comprehend or appreciate any logical explanation of differential treatment. If they see another child getting something, they feel that they should have it, too.

To help level 1 children cope with differential treatment and to facilitate their growth, you should utilize level 2 thinking:

- "Bill gets to use it today; you'll get a chance tomorrow."
- "Barb can feed the horse; you'll get a chance to do something else special."
- "We'll take turns with the Panda. This morning it's Greg's turn."
- "Yesterday, Sam was able to light the candle. Today, Billy Jean has a special job."

Even though young children will have a difficult time accepting differential treatment, it should be used because it provides an avenue for developing moral reasoning and because it enriches the curriculum and adds flexibility to your teaching.

As students mature, you can encourage their acceptance of differential treatment by having them consider other points of view and your intentions as a teacher (level 3 reasoning):

- "Manuel, you're the lucky one who gets to help Miss Alvarez today. How do you think Jamie and the rest of the students feel?"
- "Three of you won't be able to complete the project because we ran out of material. How is it going to feel to be one of the ones left out?"

- "I would like to have the whole class visit the animal shelter, but Mrs. Jones only has room for eight. How should we determine who gets to go?"

Students can probably accept differential treatment in terms of learning activities and methodology more easily than they can accept differential treatment for disciplinary measures. The concern for consistency in discipline has a wide base of support. Part of this concern can be traced to the legalistic nature of our society. Students, parents, teachers, and the general public expect equal treatment under the law. If two people are guilty of the same crime, they should get the same punishment. This issue has been clearly expressed by the Pennsylvania Task Force on Student Responsibility and Discipline:

> Certain very obvious parallels exist between our criminal justice system and the discipline system in our schools. Whether they are administered in the courtroom by the judge or in the classroom by the teacher, both systems attempt to bring about responsible behavior by carefully defining unacceptable acts and by prescribing their consequences.

> The common elements shared by the criminal justice and school discipline systems give rise to similar problems. One is the issue of consistency. A major area of controversy in our justice system centers around the broad discretion allowed in the sentencing of offenders. This considerable latitude not only results in identical violations receiving very different punishments, but also produces what many feel are mismatches between the seriousness of the offense and the severity of the penalty.

> It is not uncommon to hear students and parents criticize the application of discipline in the schools on the same basis. They assert that the rules for student conduct are ambiguous and inconsistently administered and that the penalties for breaking these rules are not applied equally to all students.

> Even though the concept of equal justice for all is often difficult to realize in the school situation, every effort should be made to assure that an evenhanded, reasonable and consistent approach to discipline is always practiced. These factors are essential if the system

is to command the respect and confidence necessary to make it work.

(Source: *Guidelines for School Discipline,* prepared by the Pennsylvania Department of Education, Commissioner's Task Force on Student Responsibility and Discipline, 1976, p. 13.)

The need for consistency when punishment is involved cannot be denied. The point that needs to be made is that at the elementary level, punishment should be a last resort when it comes to reacting to misbehavior (see Chapter 11). In most cases, what is needed is a conference during which the teacher tries to understand and possibly change the student's perception of the situation and the behavior involved. *This is a teaching situation and differential treatment should be used.*

Most of these conferences should be held privately. If a conference is held in a public situation, the student will have a much greater need to protect his ego and, thus, he will be on the defensive.

PRINCIPLE: **It is difficult to change one's position once it is stated publicly.**

Students will benefit from hearing their peers discuss a conflict situation. But it takes a special class and a highly skilled teacher to successfully discuss a conflict situation that directly involves students in the class. In most cases, it would be better to discuss the specific problem on a private basis and to have the class deal with other, less directly related social and value conflicts in class.

Comments: Most students can accept differential treatment in terms of groupings, assignments, and distribution of jobs and privileges; however, there is little acceptance by parents or students when it comes to differential treatment under the law.

Differential treatment should be used in reacting to most off-task behavior at the elementary level. This is so because students vary in their social maturity, their level of moral reasoning, and because circumstances will also differ. Therefore, what is needed to successfully use differential treatment in reacting to misbehavior is the perspective that misbehavior is an error in judgment and not a sinful act of disobedience (this idea is developed in Chapter 11). This is one reason why you don't want a long list of class rules (see Chapter 7). The more rules you have, the more legalistic you have to become. Use general rules with the emphasis on judgment, not law. This will help you avoid the use of punishment; and instead, you can stress the use of private conferences. If this is the case, then differential treatment is in order.

SUMMARY

The old saying, "Be firm, fair, and consistent," has survived for so long because it carries a great deal of truth. But there are several ways to look at consistency.

If we're talking about the use of punishment in a legalistic sense—"you broke the rule, so you're going to be punished"—then certainly all students should be treated consistently. But, at the elementary level, most disciplinary measures call for teaching, not punishment. In matters of teaching, differential treatment is preferred. Fixed responses should only be used for serious offenses or when the student is openly defying established policy.

Another way of looking at consistency is that you should have a well thought out set of beliefs and principles to guide your teaching. In this sense, consistency means that you have a reason for your behavior, you know what you're doing, you know why you're doing it, and you're able to explain your reasoning to the children. Your consistency is in your logic and rhetoric. You're also consistent in the way you handle a given child under a given condition. You hold different expectations, you use different methodologies, and you react differently depending on the circumstances. But you operate at the awareness level; you know what you're doing and why you're doing it.

You can also be consistent in that you follow through on something. If you tell a student to do something, you see that it's done. If you threaten, you're ready to carry out the threat. If you react one way, you react the same way the next time, as long as the conditions remain the same.

Being consistent is important, but so is differential treatment. *Differential treatment shows respect for individuals, enriches the students' learning opportunities, and allows for greater flexibility.*

10

Guidelines and Techniques for Reacting to Misbehavior

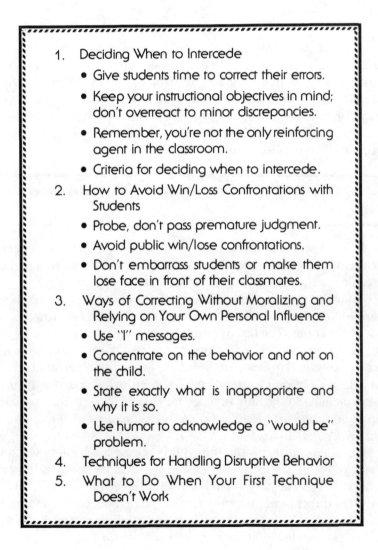

1. Deciding When to Intercede
   - Give students time to correct their errors.
   - Keep your instructional objectives in mind; don't overreact to minor discrepancies.
   - Remember, you're not the only reinforcing agent in the classroom.
   - Criteria for deciding when to intercede.
2. How to Avoid Win/Loss Confrontations with Students
   - Probe, don't pass premature judgment.
   - Avoid public win/lose confrontations.
   - Don't embarrass students or make them lose face in front of their classmates.
3. Ways of Correcting Without Moralizing and Relying on Your Own Personal Influence
   - Use "I" messages.
   - Concentrate on the behavior and not on the child.
   - State exactly what is inappropriate and why it is so.
   - Use humor to acknowledge a "would be" problem.
4. Techniques for Handling Disruptive Behavior
5. What to Do When Your First Technique Doesn't Work

DECIDING WHEN TO INTERCEDE

Teachers who have management problems are usually guilty of overreacting to minor incidents. They tend to be "quick draw" artists, nailing students for minor errors; or, they go to the other extreme, they don't see the first offender, and they nail the wrong person or wait until a minor brush fire has engulfed the class.

In reacting to off-task behavior, *you need to consciously consider when and how you should intercede.*

PRINCIPLE: **Give students time to correct their errors.**

Don't treat the student like the enemy. Believe in your students, give them enough rein to make mistakes, and give them enough time to recognize their errors and correct them.

Consider the following episode: While a teacher is conducting a lesson on homonyms, Cheryl gets up and starts walking toward the back of the room. The teacher's immediate reaction is to remind her that she's supposed to be working at her seat. Cheryl may be going after a paper towel to clean up the ink she accidentally smeared on her desk, she may be going after a pencil she left in her coat, or she may have remembered the note the secretary asked her to deliver to Sara. *Trust your students. Remember, they're doing what they think is right under the circumstances.*

Consider another situation: Bill is taking his spelling test and he's forgotten to put his spelling list away. You see the list sitting on his desk. If he's cheating, you don't want to accuse him publicly; if he's not, a direct reminder would be embarrassing. Give him time to realize his error. When he does, it will be a laughing matter instead of a blow against his character. *Give students time to correct their errors.*

PRINCIPLE: Keep your instructional objectives in mind; don't overreact to minor discrepancies.

When something is out of place, the tendency is to react immediately:

- "Steve, what's the paper doing on the floor?"
- "Who left the dictionary on the table?"
- "Your math workbooks should be put away, not on top of your desks."

Such comments stop the flow of a lesson. They direct the class's attention away from the task at hand. Keep things in perspective, and don't immediately react to off-task behavior or mislaid items. The ability to judge the severity of an act and to act accordingly is a sign of professional maturity. *Keep your objectives in mind.*

PRINCIPLE: Remember, you're not the only reinforcing agent in the classroom.

Many teachers err by trying to ignore misbehavior, hoping it will die from lack of attention. Don't forget that there are other reinforcing agents in the classroom. With a twinkle of the eye, with a raised eyebrow, or with a sly smile, another student can quietly feed the fire while you are trying to ignore the problem. Remember, you're not the only reinforcing agent in the classroom.

Picture the following: Mark has discovered that, when he pulls his wet palm across his plastic binder, it sounds like a slight gas emission. Rather than recognize the earthy humor, you choose to ignore it, hoping it will go away. That could happen, if it weren't for Al's wrinkled nose and Chuck's cherub-like grin. But it won't go away, because Mark is getting all the support he needs. *Remember: When a student acts up, others are probably egging him on. In these cases, ignoring the misbehavior probably won't work.*

When you do intercede in a case like the above, make sure you aim your remarks at all those involved, including the students who are supporting the offender as well as those directly involved. If other students in the class are reinforcing the misbehavior, then they should also bear the responsibility for it. The criteria presented in Figure 10-1 should help you determine when to intercede.

CRITERIA FOR DECIDING WHEN TO INTERCEDE

You should intercede if:

1. The misbehavior threatens anyone's health or well-being.
2. Other students begin to join in or encourage the offender.
3. The misbehavior is distracting other students and interfering with your instructional objectives.
4. The offender is not meeting a behavior commitment that was previously made.
5. The misbehavior is interfering with other classes or could lead to P.R. problems with parents or staff.
6. Other students observed the misbehavior and are looking at you, waiting to see what you are going to do.

If you have to intercede, your reaction should reflect the severity of the act. If at all possible, postpone any direct confrontation with the student until after the lesson or until you can do so privately.

Figure 10-1

Comments: During the homonym lesson, when Cheryl got up and started walking to the back of the room, you should have been curiously aware of the situation, but to intercede would have been inappropriate. The other students don't seem bothered by her movement, she seems to have an objective in mind, and she hasn't been out of her seat for a long time. If you intercede, you draw the class's attention away from the lesson. You can hope that each and every student in the class is paying avid attention to your lesson, but chances are, one or two students will be daydreaming or momentarily distracted. Don't overreact when one or two students are momentarily off-task.

HOW TO AVOID WIN/LOSE CONFRONTATIONS WITH STUDENTS

As I have indicated, the first principle of managing a classroom is to believe that the children want to do what's right. If George is whispering when you think he shouldn't be, force yourself to believe he may have a good reason for whispering. If Sue and Mary are passing notes during study period, consider that they may have a legitimate reason for doing so. If Jim turns around in line and slugs the boy behind him, it may be a justifiable response under the circumstances (at least Jim may see it as justifiable). Misbehavior has to be situationally defined. Don't be premature in passing judgment.

PRINCIPLE: **Probe, don't pass premature judgment.**

Don't immediately condemn a student's behavior. Probe before you pass judgment. Expect the child to have a good reason for his behavior, at least a good reason from his point of view.

- "George, can I help you?"
- "Mary, do you need to talk to Sue now?"
- "Hold on, Jim, what's the problem?"

Don't be too quick to pass judgment. Give yourself time to see what's happening and give students time to correct their own errors.

Trusting your students is the key. If you believe that the students act from a positive base, both your verbal and nonverbal behaviors will communicate this trust. If you believe that the students want to learn and want to do what's right, then you'll try to find a reason to explain their apparent misbehavior. *If the students sense your faith in them, they will react by fulfilling your expectations.*

Questions such as the above seek clarification. They stem from the belief that students have a good reason for what they're doing. They reflect the philosophy that people are basically good and want to do what's right.

When you probe, you should be honestly seeking information. Don't kid yourself by thinking you're probing when you ask rhetorical questions which accuse or point a guilty finger.

- "Jim, should you be doing that?"
- "Sally, is this the time to be cleaning your desk?"
- "Class, are we supposed to be talking?"

These are not probes, they don't seek clarification, and in these cases the answers are known and predictable. Questions such as these can be used at times to shape student behavior, but when used they represent a negative, coercive approach, an approach which relies on power.

"**Fair minded teachers who make the basic assumption that children are trustworthy are more likely to teach them to have attitudes of dependability and responsibility.**"—Dreikurs

---

Avoid using "why" questions when you seek clarification.

- "Pete, why are you doing that?"
- "Alice, why did you leave the glue bottle out?"
- "Beverly, why do you have two books on your desk?"

The "why" question is usually interpreted as an accusation, a fault-finding remark. The student will often read a negative message into the question.

- "Pete, you dummy, why are you doing that?"
- "Alice, you're so careless, why did you leave the glue bottle out?"
- "Beverly, can't you remember the rules, why do you have two books out?"

"Why" questions usually spawn defensive behaviors. If a student has obviously forgotten a rule, it is better to quickly point it out. Consider the examples in Figure 10-2.

PRINCIPLE: **Avoid public win/lose confrontations.**

When you confront a student publicly, you run a tremendous risk of losing face with your students. In almost every audience situation, you're going to be the loser. If you come down hard on a child or punish the child in front of the class, some students are going to see you as being unfair or too harsh. Others will see you as being too soft, or an easy mark. Few will look at you as being fair. Even if they do, your action will have negative ripple effects. Other students will indirectly feel threatened—they may be next.

A direct "task-oriented" reminder does not carry the negative personal overtones.	The accusing "why" question spawns negative student reactions.
"Pete, you're supposed to be collecting the blocks, not stacking them."	"Pete, why are you doing that?"
"Alice, if you're through with the glue bottle, make sure it gets put away."	"Alice, why did you leave the glue bottle out?"
"Beverly, only one book please, unless you have a special reason for using two."	"Beverly, why do you have two books on your desk?"

Figure 10-2

With young children, you may be able to confront students publicly without running as great a risk, but the power play still unnecessarily invites negative side effects.

Think about the following situations:

1. Another student accuses Jim of cheating during the spelling test. He evidently has written his hard words on his fingers.
2. A paper airplane whizzes across the room. When you turn around, Berta has a very guilty look.
3. Billy is playing in his desk with what looks like a ball of clay. He is supposed to be listening to Betty's report on Chile.

In each of the above cases, you have options. How would you handle the situations? If you confront a child in front of the class, you're inviting the child to deny your accusations. If the child doesn't try to save face, you end up publicly embarrassing the child. Either way, you're not helping the child build a positive self-concept and you're not endearing yourself to the rest of the class.

An all too common example of public embarrassment is the habit of calling on a student who isn't paying attention. You're trying to shape his behavior by publicly embarrassing him. You know he probably can't answer your question. You can just as easily shape the student's behavior by calling on a child sitting next to the culprit. The close call will bring the offender around without public embarrassment.

If, when you publicly confront a child, the child tries to save face and denies the act, then you've got another win/lose situation. Whenever you argue with a child in front of the class, you run a tremendous risk of appearing unfair. Such a clash always appears to be a David and Goliath affair. Being right may not make you a winner. If you don't allow the student to argue his side, or defend himself against your accusation, you appear unfair. Even when you have a strong case, a public win/lose confrontation will probably tarnish your teaching effectiveness.

PRINCIPLE: **Don't embarrass students or make them lose face in front of their classmates.**

When you confront a child, try to detour the child rather than block him. If you tell me I can't do something or I have to do something, you're giving me a direct challenge. I'm going to tell you to go jump in a lake or, in some way, I'm going to protect my ego.

I can still remember my third grade teacher telling me I had to sing. A direct challenge: I had to sing. At that point, there was no way she could make me sing. Hitting my knuckles with a double ruler only increased my conviction to "win" at any cost, as well as eliminating any question as to whom the class was backing.

In a situation of this type, you want to capture rather than coerce. If you try to coerce, you should provide a detour or a way for the child to save face without forcing a win/lose confrontation. Figure 10-3 compares a set of detour statements with blocking statements.

Detour Statements	Blocking Statements
"Sam, this is Jim's turn. You can have your chance in a minute."	"Quit talking, Sam."
"Well, Alice, you can either join in now or you can discuss it with me after school today."	"I'm sorry, Alice, you are going to square-dance."
"Sarah, we need it quiet in this area. If you need to talk with Sue, please go to the back of the room."	"Sarah, you can't talk during reading."

"Dick, if you are not going to join in, would you please sit quietly and we'll talk after class?"	"Dick, open that book and sing."

Figure 10-3

Comments: If and when you decide to intercede, make sure you try to avoid a public confrontation. Remember to detour the student, giving him a way to save face. Consciously embarrassing a child or exposing the child's ignorance or lack of ability is abusing your leadership role.

WAYS OF CORRECTING WITHOUT MORALIZING AND RELYING ON YOUR OWN PERSONAL INFLUENCE

When a student is distracting you or causing you concern, make sure you recognize that it's your problem. You're the only one who is bothered. Notice the difference in emphasis in the statements in Figure 10-4.

I Message	You Message
"I'm really discouraged when you change names with a substitute."	"You know you shouldn't act up like that. What's the matter with you?"
"I'm really worried that the paint will get spilled if you leave it there."	"You should move the paint. You're going to spill it if you leave it there."
"Would you clear your desk? I'm afraid the material will be distracting."	"Please clear your desk. You should not be playing with anything on your desk."

Figure 10-4

PRINCIPLE: Use "I messages."

A student can't deny your feelings and will more than likely be responsive to them. But a student can deny your prediction that he is going to do something wrong. He can feel you're being too picky if you tell him there's a better way. And he can feel you're being unfair if you put the blame on him before he's guilty. Remember to acknowledge your part of the problem. You're the one who's concerned!

In sharing your feelings, it's also important to provide a rationale for why something bothers you. Young children will cooperate because they want to please the teacher, but this doesn't last for long and it shouldn't be relied upon. In terms of social behavior, the goal is rational decision making. You want students to cooperate because they understand why cooperation is important. When you intercede, be specific, concentrate on the behavior, and tell exactly why it's not desirable.

PRINCIPLE: **Concentrate on the behavior and not on the child.**

A task focused comment forces you to name the undesirable behavior. Compare the statements in Figure 10-5.

Task Focused Comments	Child Focused Comments
"Jimmy, it's distracting when you throw wads of paper like that at the garbage can."	"Jimmy, you're causing problems again. Don't do that."
"Mary, your clicking your pen bothers me and I'm sure it bothers others, too."	"Mary, are you nervous or something? Quit clicking your pen."
"Pete, you can play with the clay during free time. Put it away now, you should be working on your math."	"What's the matter with you, Pete? You know you're not supposed to be playing with that clay now."

Figure 10-5

Clarity has been shown to be the number one teacher trait that has a positive and consistent relationship with student achievement (Rosenshine and Furst). Clarity was also found to be the most important variable in terms of successfully responding to misbehavior (Kounin). Kounin has indicated that teachers who are specific in their reactions get more conformity to class standards and have fewer class disruptions when compared with teachers who are general or don't give reasons for their reactions.

High Clarity	Low Clarity
"Johnny, put that clay away. It distracts me."	"Johnny, you know better than that."
"Salina, you can read after you finish your math."	"Salina, get to work."
"Karen, sit down. With all this material on the desks, we can't risk so much commotion."	"Karen, please get in your seat."

Figure 10-6

Compare the statements in Figure 10-6. An effective technique is to ask the child, "What are you doing?" Follow this question with, "What should you be doing?"

PRINCIPLE: **State exactly what is inappropriate and why it is so.**

PRINCIPLE: **Use humor to acknowledge a "would be" problem.**

A little humor can turn a "would be" discipline case into a lighthearted situation (see Figure 10-7). The message can be communicated without a confrontation or nasty scene.

Use of Humor	Direct Confrontation
1. In response to an airplane flying across the room:	
"Now hear this, all future launches are cancelled."	"Who threw that airplane?"

Figure 10-7

2.   In response to a talkative group of students:

Teacher goes to the   "You're talking too much
board and writes: If you don't quiet down,
                             you'll have to make up the
AFTER SCHOOL TALKING time after school.
CLUB

Pres. _____

1. _____

2. _____

3.   In response to two students pushing in line:

"You guys getting ready   "Take your seats. When
for the Golden   you're ready to line up
Gloves ?"   like gentlemen, you may."

Figure 10-7 (cont'd)

Comments: In reacting to off-task behavior, try to tone down the situation. Use "I messages" and humor to get your message across, avoid frequent use of moralizing, and avoid child focused comments. Strive for clarity. State exactly what behavior is undesirable and why.

TECHNIQUES FOR HANDLING DISRUPTIVE BEHAVIOR

ITEM 146.   Provide an Opportunity for Students to Settle Their Own Problems

If two or three students are having an argument, tell them to go to the corner of the room and work it out. Ask them to come back when they have reached a plan and tell you what they've decided.

Carmen Heltne
Lake Mills, Iowa

ITEM 147.   June Box

A box, much like a ballot box in design, can be decorated and conspicuously labeled, "June Box." If students persist in playing with items that are distracting, the items can be deposited in the June Box. As the name indicates, the box isn't opened until June. A Friday Box may be more appropriate for younger children.

ITEM 148.   Identify Positive Behavior

In the primary grades, you can shape student behavior by complimenting a student who is setting a positive example: "I like the way that John is sitting quietly." This reinforces positive behavior and has a desirable "ripple effect" on the other students.

In the intermediate grades, this can have a negative effect. If you compliment a child for his good behavior, others will wonder why they weren't recognized, and you open the door for negative peer pressure. Students will begin to tease the "good student" for being an "apple polisher" and "teacher's pet."

Jane Dunbar
Miles-Sabula, Iowa

ITEM 149.   Playground Strategy

When students become involved in a situation where they are fighting or at least violently disagreeing, take those involved aside and calmly question them about what each of them can do to improve the situation. Don't dwell on how the argument started or who is to blame, for this is a dead-end road. Focus on ways to better cope with the situation if it happens again and decide on what they should do right now.

Another technique is to have each student involved in the situation write down his view of the happening as it occurred. This gives those involved a chance to "cool down," and a chance to think about the situation.

After reading each version, you can discuss how the situation could have been avoided and what could be done to cure the problem. It's a good idea to draw up a contract in terms of what to do now and have all those concerned sign it. You could agree to meet the next day to evaluate how the plan seems to be working.

Mrs. Patricia Arthaud
Oelwein, Iowa

The writing technique is also useful if a student brings in a complaint after recess. If a student comes in after recess and explodes about some problem, tell the student to sit down and write it out. Tell him you will read the incident and decide whether to handle it individually or in a class meeting. It is important to get back to the student and follow up on his complaint.

Mrs. Mabel English
Clinton, Iowa

ITEM 150.   Letter to Parents (held until needed)

If a student commits an obvious misdeed, hold a private conference with the student in an area where you will not be disturbed or overheard. Tell the child to write a letter to his parents telling exactly what he did. When this is done to your satisfaction, tell the child that you will not send the letter unless the situation is not corrected or happens again. Impress upon the child that you don't expect him to do it again and you hope you don't have to send the letter.

Mrs. Irene Herteen
Blakesburg, Iowa

ITEM 151.   Write Five Alternatives

When a child misbehaves, talk to him about what happened. Listen to his version of what happened and talk about the situation that developed. Did his actions get the desired results? What did he think would happen when he did what he did? Was it a good situation that developed?

When you've talked about these things, have the student write five good reasons why he should not have done what he did and five alternatives that he will work on so that it doesn't happen again. Whether he will try to change attitudes or actions, you now have a list of goals toward which the student is going to work. Have the student concentrate on one modification at a time. Check with the student at the beginning or end of each day to evaluate his progress.

Mrs. Pauline Dannenbring
Denmark, Iowa

ITEM 152.   "That's Number One!"

When you meet with a student, you might confront him with the fact that he seems to be seeking special attention. If the child seems to recognize that this is the case, you could ask him how many times he may want special attention during the day. Usually he'll respond with, "I don't know." You might suggest 10 or 15 times. Usually the student will feel that's too high. After an agreement is reached, each time the child attracts attention to himself, you just respond by saying, "Johnny, that's number one!" and so on.

ITEM 153.   A Timer

When a child has difficulty getting to work, discuss the problem with him and get a commitment about what he feels he can do, and how long it will take him to do it. Set a timer accordingly and place it on the child's desk. This serves as a reminder and also gives him a definite challenge to beat.

Team III
Prairie View Elementary
Cedar Rapids, Iowa

ITEM 154.   Use Data to Chart Student Progress

This idea combines two basic educational principles: (1) Students develop along a continuum. You shouldn't expect instant success, but you should work for successive approximations. (2) Success is the greatest motivator. If the students can see that they are making progress, they will work much harder toward the given goal.

If students are shouting out too much, give them a chart to mark each time they forget to use their soft voices. Divide the day into four blocks of time and keep count of how many times the undesirable behavior occurs. Chart this on a graph for a week. With this data providing a base line, meet with the students involved and discuss the behavior and how many times it occurred during each of the four blocks of time. Help the students decide on a reasonable goal for the next week (it's important to try a small step so that they can meet success). Follow this procedure until the undesirable behavior has been modified successfully.

Dorothy Bailie
Clarinda, Iowa

ITEM 155.   Behavior Modification Contract

For individual students having difficulty adjusting to school rules, use a Behavior Modification Contract Plan. The rules that the student has difficulty in following are listed. A hierarchy of difficulty is made from the list—from hardest to easiest. Use the easiest rule to follow as the starting point.

The contract is discussed with the student until it is completely understood and agreeable to the child. Copies of the contract are made available for signature and retention by parents, administrator, teacher, and child. See Figure 10-8 for a sample contract.

George Holland
Sergeant Bluff, Iowa

Behavior Modification Contract

I, _____ , will try to control my actions by
　　　(student's name)

_____ during the two-week period
　　(area in need of improvement)

beginning _____ and ending _____ . During
this time, I will evaluate my actions with my teacher every
half-day—at noon and at the end of the day. If I have

achieved, I will receive a _____ as proof of my
　　　　　　　　　　　　　　　(sticker, star, card)
achievements.

　　If, during this time, I have shown improvement, I will

receive _____ . If I fail to improve, I will meet with
　　　(material or academic reward)
my parents and teacher to rewrite my contract in a way
that will allow me to show improvement. At the end of a

successful period, I will continue to _____
　　　　　　　　　　　　　　　　　　　(area of shown improvement)
and add the next area of improvement listed below, in
order to make myself a successful student in my home,
school, and community.

Areas of improvement　　　Signed.

1.　　　　　　　　　　　　_____
　　　　　　　　　　　　　　(Student's signature)

2.　　　　　　　　　　　　_____
　　　　　　　　　　　　　　(Teacher's signature)

3.　　　　　　　　　　　　_____
　　　　　　　　　　　　　　(Parent's signature)

4.　　　　　　　　　　　　_____
　　　　　　　　　　　　　　(Administrator's signature)

Figure 10-8

Comments: This section presents a number of techniques for handling disruptive behavior. The ideas are recommended for use, but only under certain conditions. Generally speaking, the most effective way to handle disruptive behavior is to talk privately with the offender. This should be tried several times before employing most of the techniques presented in this section. Remember: The most effective way to change behavior is to change perceptions. A June Box, writing alternatives, and behavior modification contracts can contribute to an adversary relationship. If used, they should be used sparingly.

WHAT TO DO WHEN YOUR FIRST TECHNIQUE DOESN'T WORK

There is no sure-fire technique to which all children will respond. The effective teacher has a number of alternatives. There will be times when your first idea doesn't work. What do you do next?

What does a mechanic do when the wrench he has won't budge a bolt? Get a bigger wrench? That's not the only solution. Tapping the end of the bolt with a hammer might help, or applying some rust solvent might do the trick.

So it goes with a teacher. If the first technique doesn't work, you don't necessarily have to apply more pressure; you might try a different attack.

Say you have two boys who constantly race to see who can be the first one in his desk after recess. You ask them to stop, but they continue. What do you do?

1. Assign the boys permanent places in line and have the class line up before they come in after recess.

2. Move one of the desks closer to the door so that there is no contest.

3. Give one of the boys a responsibility (hold the door open, distribute papers, hand out workbooks).

4. Explain your concerns to the boys in more detail (it gives the appearance that you have an unruly room; if everyone did it you would be concerned about safety; that kind of movement just makes you nervous).

5. Make sure you get back to your class by the end of recess and position yourself in a conspicuous spot to help the boys "remember" not to run.

The key is flexibility. Don't just get a bigger wrench. If you rely on power alone, you'll soon find yourself in an adversary relationship with your class. Once that happens, you have lost the battle. The students can be very creative and they have fewer constraints in terms of what they can or can't do once they see you as the enemy.

SUMMARY

This chapter stresses the importance of teaching at the awareness level. You're the master of the ship, you need to stay in control, you need to avoid merely reacting to misbehavior out of habit. This chapter provides criteria for deciding when to intercede, alternatives for avoiding win/lose confrontations with students, and specific techniques for reacting to misbehavior.

11

Punishment and Its Appropriate Use

1. Selecting the Appropriate Punishment
    - Confer with students; avoid other punitive measures.
    - Limit your punitive reactions to natural consequences.
2. Important Do's and Don'ts Regarding the Use of Punishment
    - Punishment is a legitimate teaching device.
    - Punishment is appropriate when learning has to be immediate.
    - Avoid harsh punishment.
    - Aggression teaches aggression.
    - Many negative side effects are associated with the use of punishment.
    - Punishment does not solve the child's problem.
    - Always explain why you use a punishment.
    - Avoid delayed or long-term punishment.
    - Don't use mass punishment unless the group is either condoning or supporting the misbehavior.
    - Don't use exclusion from learning experiences as a punishment.
    - Punishing the remedial child confirms his feelings of failure and inadequacy.
3. The Use of Isolation and Systematic Exclusion
    - Isolation should be used to protect the welfare of the students and not as a punishment.
4. Suspensions and Corporal Punishment
    - Restraint and corporal punishment are not the same.
5. Criteria for Evaluating Disciplinary Measures

SELECTING THE APPROPRIATE PUNISHMENT

Professional terms are designed to clarify concepts and eliminate unnecessary descriptions; however, they can provide a short circuit as well as a short cut. Punishment is one of those words that can short circuit or muddle our thinking because it covers a whole array of reactions. To clarify and hopefully sharpen thinking, three separate categories of punishment are discussed in this chapter.

1. Changing Perceptions.

If you talk with students and try to help them understand why they shouldn't behave in a given way, you're trying to change their perceptions. If you keep students after school to talk with them about a problem, you're trying to clarify the problem and change perceptions. Here the stress is on talking with the students versus keeping them after school to merely "put in time."

PRINCIPLE: **Confer with students; avoid other punitive measures.**

In a comprehensive study, Brophy and Evertson reported:

> *The most effective forms of punishments were not really punishments at all. Instead they were actions such as keeping the child after school or arranging for an individual conference with him in order to discuss his misbehavior and come to some kind of agreement about how the problem was to be solved.*

A private conference is an effective technique for working with individual students in trying to change their perceptions. It is important that the conference be private. Audience situations should be avoided. Conferences should be on a private, one-to-one basis.

You should not dominate the talking in such a conference. If you do, chances are you're moralizing. Telling is seldom an effective technique for changing perceptions.

Encourage the student to actively participate by using some of the techniques listed in Figure 11-1.

Conference Techniques to Involve Students

1. Ask the student to describe how he sees the situation. **Don't contradict his views or imply that they are inaccurate.** They are his views.

2. Ask the student to **hypothesize** about how the others involved might view the situation.

3. Encourage the student to describe how he feels about the situation. **Use a perception check.**
   - "Did that make you want revenge?"
   - "Did you feel cheated, or were you just mad?"

4. Ask the child to **hypothesize** about how the others feel now.

5. Ask the student to **suggest other ways** in which the problem could have been settled.

6. If the student is reluctant to respond, suggest how the others could have felt, how they could have perceived the situation, other ways to react, and **ask him to repeat what you have said.**

7. Ask the student if he has any ideas about **what should happen now.**

8. Ask the student to **predict what will happen next** if the same course of action is followed. Ask whether he thinks the others want that to happen.

9. Ask the student **how he thinks you feel** about what happened.

Figure 11-1

In these conferences, it is important to recognize the student's emotions and the fact that we all have different perspectives on a situation and its consequences. Remember that, as a teacher, you may not feel that being called "bird legs" or "hummingbird chest" is anything worth fighting over, but to the student it's a completely different matter.

It's important to remember that, viewed from the student's perspective, he did what he thought was best.

You should tell the student how you feel and why you are bothered by his actions, but make sure you express your own feelings (see "I Messages" in Chapter 10).

Stress the fact that *the problem arises out of different views of the situation.* Have the student try to see the other's position. Work on alternative reactions and *make sure the conference ends with a plan of action,* even if that plan is merely to meet again and discuss the problem some more.

In terms of punishment, a private conference after school, during recess, or during class does not force the adversary role inherent in more punitive measures.

2. Natural Consequences.

Suffering a natural consequence is the second form of punishment. If a child abuses a privilege, it is a natural consequence that he will lose that privilege. For example, if a child can't go by himself to the library without goofing around, it is natural that he will only go to the library under direct supervision. If he is playing with clay when he's supposed to be reading, being forced to put the clay away or having it taken away is a natural consequence. If his friends and he push and shove in line, it's a natural consequence that they will be separated and assigned permanent spots in line.

In most cases, when the punitive reactions you use follow logically from the misbehavior, most students will not see you as being terribly unfair; thus, when you use natural consequences as your punishment, you do not run a high risk of creating an adversary or enemy relationship with your class.

PRINCIPLE: **Limit your punitive reactions to natural consequences.**

---

3. Arbitrary Punishments.

If you use arbitrary punishments which do not follow naturally, many students will see you as being unfair. If this occurs repeatedly, you'll develop an adversary relationship and become fair game for cheating and other headaches. If, as a consequence of talking too much in class, a child has to write 50 sentences ("I will not talk in school"), the sentence writing does not follow naturally and it is an arbitrary punishment. If the child loses his art period because he didn't complete his math assignment, this would also be an arbitrary punishment.

The three categories (perception change, natural consequences, and arbitrary punishments) overlap considerably. If a student sharpened a crayon in the pencil sharpener, you might keep him after school to help the custodian clean the sharpener. This is a natural consequence because he messed up the sharpener. You're also working on perceptions by showing what a crayon does to the inside of a sharpener.

Making distinctions among the three types of punishment is helpful in terms of how you administer the punishment.

1. If you paddle a child, you are definitely using an arbitrary punishment. It is never a natural consequence.

2. If you make a child sit with his head on the desk for five minutes, that's usually an arbitrary punishment.

3. If two students are talking and you decide to move their seats to separate them, that's a natural consequence of their talking.

4. If a child is using a jump rope at recess as a whip, and chasing other children, taking the rope away would be a natural consequence.

5. If a child loses the privilege of taking a rope out at recess because he was talking in class, that's an arbitrary punishment. If the child is sent out so that the teacher can talk with him privately, this would fall under the category of trying to change perceptions; however, if the teacher does all the talking and merely gives the student a tongue lashing, then it would be an arbitrary punishment.

As a general rule of thumb, the use of natural consequences and the attempt to change perceptions are more desirable than the use of arbitrary punishments. This is particularly true when reacting to the typical child in a public situation.

Comments: In this section, stress was placed on reacting to undesirable behavior by trying to change perceptions. A distinction was made between punitive acts which follow as a natural consequence of a student's behavior, and those which are selected arbitrarily. If you have to use punitive measures, try to use natural consequences.

Avoid arbitrary punishments because students will see you as unfair and this will promote an adversary relationship between you and your class.

IMPORTANT DO'S AND DON'TS REGARDING THE USE OF PUNISHMENT

PRINCIPLE: **Punishment is a legitimate teaching device.**

A swat on the behind, a firm shake, isolation in a "time out area," being "benched," and other punishments are legitimate teaching devices. They have their place when a change of behavior is needed immediately or when someone's well-being is threatened.

I can remember giving my two-year-old son a key case to keep him occupied while my wife and I shopped for a refrigerator. It wasn't long before I found Mike trying to put a key into an electrical outlet. My reaction was swift and to the point. I gave him a good slap on the hand, knocking the key away from the outlet. The message was clear: "No! That's dangerous. Don't ever do it again." This was one of those cases where the punishment was appropriate, because learning had to be immediate.

PRINCIPLE: **Punishment is appropriate when the learning has to be immediate.**

Punishment puts you in an adversary relationship with your students and should be used only when time is of the essence. When you force an adversary role, you effectively close the door for cooperative problem solving. You also place students in a defensive position, and any change in perceptions becomes highly unlikely. Furthermore, when you force an adversary role, you increase the likelihood that students will see you as unfair; thus, you become a target for revenge.

Punishment has its place but should be used sparingly. It should never become the standard reaction to misbehavior.

PRINCIPLE: **Avoid harsh punishment.**

With confident and able students, mild criticism associates positively with student achievement. With all types of students, harsh punishment has a consistent negative relationship with achievement. Telling a child that his answer is wrong or correcting the way a student holds a pencil are necessary parts of teaching. Mild criticism is needed, but harsh punishment is undesirable.

You can be firm without being harsh. Kounin (1970) used the following characteristics to define firmness:

1. A clear break in the ongoing classroom activity: The teacher changes his location in the room, using a tone of voice which clearly conveys that the activity is undesirable.

2. Establishing eye contact with the offender: The teacher looks right at the misbehaving student and maintains eye contact while correcting the youngster. The teacher also maintains eye contact for a short time after the child has been reprimanded.

3. Movement toward the offender.

4. Physically assisting the offender: The teacher moves a chair or leads the student by the arm.

It is important to stress again (see Chapter 1) that Kounin's findings indicate that effective classroom management is not determined by the skillful meting out of punishment or the skillful reaction to misbehavior. Instead, the key is how successful you are in avoiding misbehavior. Try to be in control. Engineer, don't just react.

PRINCIPLE: **Aggression teaches aggression.**

In classrooms where teachers frequently exhibit anger and punitiveness, students react by exhibiting more disruptive, restless, off-task behavior. When you punish a child, you present a real threat to the other children. The increased anxiety often surfaces in more disruptive behavior. Aggression teaches aggression. When you punish, you model the type of behavior you want to stop.

PRINCIPLE: **Many negative side effects are associated with the use of punishment.**

When you administer punishment, there will be negative ripple effects on other students. Whether you use natural consequences or an arbitrary punishment, many students will see you as being unfair. The students will have a different picture of the situation. They will view the consequences of the undesirable behavior in a different light, and they will have a different view of your reaction. Some students will see your punishment as too light and will think that you're an easy mark. Others will see you as too harsh and will judge you as unfair. If students view a teacher as unfair, they tend to cheat more and cooperate less. For these reasons, you should try to avoid using punitive measures.

PRINCIPLE: **Punishment does not solve the child's problem.**

If a negative consequence is powerful enough, it will subdue the behavior. The roots of the behavior still exist even though the student is kept at bay. Students in a quiet class ruled by fear are seldom well disciplined, they are just intimidated. As Hymes has indicated, the mark of a good teacher is not how quiet you keep the pond, it is what you do with the ripples.

When you use punishment in bringing order to a class, you're solving *your problem, your need for a quiet class.* You're not dealing with the causes of the students' unrest and/or misbehavior.

PRINCIPLE: **Always explain why you use a punishment.**

The student should be told specifically why he is being punished. Too frequently, the students see the punishment as a personal rejection rather than as the logical consequences of misconduct. You should make a personal contact with the student as soon as possible after the punishment has been administered. It is important to show your concern for the student while rejecting his misbehavior.

PRINCIPLE: **Avoid delayed or long-term punishment.**

With punishment, time is important. Punishment should be swift and to the point. Extended punishments allow bad feelings to fester. We all have selective memories and we each perceive situations differently. During an extended punishment, students have a tendency to generate many negative feelings about you, the situation, and themselves.

PRINCIPLE: Don't use mass punishment unless the group is either condoning or supporting the misbehavior.

If the other students are laughing at a child's antics or are in some way reinforcing his misbehavior, the group should be addressed. Work on their perceptions. Help them to see why the misbehavior is undesirable. The group is reinforcing the misbehavior and needs attention.

When the class is supporting or reinforcing misbehavior, be slow to discipline or react with punishment to the misbehaving child. With class support, it could be possible that the student who is clowning around is acting as the agent of the class. He is providing a release of tension that may be building between the class and you, or between the class and some part of your program. If you sense that this is the case, try to initiate dialogue with the students to see where the problem lies.

There will be other situations in which many students seem to be unruly all at once. Again, be slow to punish. Stop and explain your concern. Encourage discussion of the problem and ask the students to suggest solutions.

In any case, avoid mass punishment, for it is one of the quickest ways to develop an adversary relationship with your class.

PRINCIPLE: Don't use exclusion from learning experiences as a punishment.

Don't exclude children from exciting learning experiences unless there is a logical reason for doing so. Your children have an unconditional right to learn. They're your students. Providing exciting learning experiences should not be a reward for good behavior but should be an unconditional part of their schooling experience.

With some children you will want to use an exciting experience as a contingency to motivate (see Chapter 13). In these cases, if a student doesn't perform as agreed, he doesn't get the reward. But this is an individual contract, and you are not excluding a student from a learning experience as punishment.

In some cases, students will be excluded from an activity as a natural consequence of their behavior. The key is that exclusion from an exciting learning experience should not be used as a negative contingency to punish a child.

PRINCIPLE: **Punishing a remedial child confirms his feelings of failure and inadequacy.**

Punishment should only be used with children who are socially healthy, not those who are remedial in social development. This principle deals with the use of punishment as a reaction to misbehavior and not as part of a contingency management contract (see Chapter 13).

When you react with punishment, you reinforce or confirm the student's negative feelings of failure and inadequacy. The child with severe behavior problems needs the most help. Punishment does not help, it does not provide direction toward solving the problem. This type of child really needs work on perceptions. They need to see themselves and their relationships with others in a different light. With remedial cases, changing perceptions takes considerable time and skill. The ability to do this is one of the key differences between the skilled professional educator and the warm body off the street.

Comments: In this section, a distinction was made between punitive acts which follow as a natural consequence of a student's behavior and those selected arbitrarily. Under most conditions, the use of natural consequences is more desirable. Eleven principles for using punishment have been presented. Stress was placed on avoiding harsh punitive responses. A case was made for merely conferring with students and trying to change perceptions, rather than forcing an adversary relationship by using punitive measures.

THE USE OF ISOLATION AND SYSTEMATIC EXCLUSION

There will be days when some students are so difficult to handle that they need to be isolated for the well-being of the teacher, the rest of the class, and the child himself.

Removing the student may be defeating your purposes in terms of trying to keep the youngster at work and progressing toward desired educational goals, but trying to deal with the student under the given conditions may be like knocking your head against the wall. The end result of trying to stay with the child and trying to keep him involved in the activity may find the child, you, and the rest of the class worse for the wear. Any learning that results will probably be negative learning.

When a child is taxing your patience to the limit, some type of isolation may be needed. Note: The reason for isolation is the welfare of the rest of the class. Isolation is not being recommended as a punishment.

PRINCIPLE: **Isolation should be used to protect the welfare of the students and not as a punishment.**

Isolation provides time for the student to calm down and time for the teacher to gather his wits and come up with a better strategy for handling the situation. In most cases of in-class isolation, the child can return if he feels he can do so without creating further problems.

When you punish a child by using isolation, you're using an extended punishment. If a child has to sit in the corner for 10 minutes, he has a lot of time to generate negative thoughts about you, the other students, and himself. In this situation, "putting in time" is not protecting the welfare of other students but it is being used as a negative contingency to try to shape the student's behavior. This is a very questionable practice because of its potential for negative side effects.

Timeout Areas

Room arrangements should provide various ways to partially or completely isolate a student. These areas can be used when you anticipate difficulty, rather than as a reaction to misbehavior.

Consider the following in developing a variety of isolation areas:

1. Hanging streamers from the ceiling (see Item 51). Woven materials, crepe paper streamers, and butcher paper can be hung from a wire stretched across the room.

2. Use individual carpet squares to identify an area (see Item 25).

3. If you can get a supply of small boxes, these can be painted, decorated, and used to store interest centers. They can be stacked to make portable walls that can isolate a desk or student office.

4. Cardboard from large refrigerator boxes can be used to make standing screens. Smaller boxes can be used on desks (see Item 26).

5. A pegboard or lattice work of some type can be attached to the side of a table. This can serve as a workshop area (see Item 32), or as a place to hang student work. It also provides a partial visual screen for a student work area.

Steps to Follow in Sending a Child to a Timeout Area

1. Warn the child. Let the child know that he is reaching the limits of your tolerance and that if his behavior continues he'll be asked to go to the timeout area.

2. When you send the child to a timeout area, explain your reasons very explicitly. Be brief and to the point because you may be feeding the child's need for attention.

3. Tell the student exactly how long he will have to stay in the area and give him the alternative to return earlier if he can do so without disturbing the others. If you merely tell the child that he can return when he is ready, you open the door for a battle of wills. The student may decide to see just how long you'll let him stay, forcing you to play your hand. This kind of adversary relationship should be avoided.

4. Whenever a child is sent to an isolation area, follow his return to the class with a private conference. In that conference, have the child verbalize why he went to the area and discuss alternative ways in which the problem could have been resolved. Try to be as encouraging and supportive as possible.

Isolating the child in the room is much preferred over sending the child out into the hall or to the principal's office. In the room, you can easily monitor the child's behavior, you're not spreading the problem out into the building, and the student's return to class is less conspicuous.

Systematic Exclusion

When timeout does not do the job and you need to remove the student completely, you still want to avoid a harsh punitive confrontation. Systematic exclusion provides this safety valve. It is a preplanned strategy worked out with the principal, the parents, and the student. When a teacher realizes that he has a child so socially handicapped that he represents a severe threat to the welfare of the class, the teacher should arrange a meeting of the staff members who come in contact with the child. The purpose of such a meeting would be to develop a school plan for helping the child.

Systematic exclusion may be one solution to consider. Systematic exclusion is a plan that should be established cooperatively between the staff and the parents involved for the temporary removal of the child from the school. If the child is having a hard day, he may have to go home for the rest of the morning or the rest of the day, whichever has been agreed upon as the best length of time. If the parents work, babysitting arrangements would have to be made. In using this system, follow the procedure listed below:

1. The parents should be contacted (this should not be the initial contact with the parents). They should be informed that systematic exclusion is going to be used and exactly what this means and why such severe measures are being taken.

2. The procedure should be explained to the child. A signal should be developed so that there is no need for a verbal exchange when the student is to leave the room (a yellow card could serve as a warning to the child; a red card would mean that he must immediately leave for the office).

3. The problem of what the student will do when he comes to the office should be considered. The office should react in a neutral manner. The child is handicapped by his behavior problem. When he is sent to the office, he has reached his limit and/or the teacher's tolerance level. He should either rest in the office or he should be sent directly home. If it is decided that, when he reports to the office, he

is to rest until he feels he can control himself in the room, there should be an agreed upon set of guidelines for how other teachers, the secretaries, and anyone else involved will react to the child's presence in the office.

4. If, after returning to the room, he receives another red card and reports to the office, then it is probably best to contact the parents and have him picked up by them or by the babysitter.

The important element of this strategy is that the child is handled as a handicapped individual. The teacher does not throw a fit and verbally chastise the child but merely signals that his behavior has reached a point where it is necessary for him to remove himself from the room until he can work within established limits.

This signal can be privately agreed upon. It applies to a special case and the rest of the class does not have to be involved.

These measures may seem harsh. Certainly you want the child to be in the room where he can get the needed practice on how to handle himself; certainly you want to work with the child and have him set realistic goals related to his behavior for each day; and certainly you're going to use positive reinforcement to try to change his behavior. But, the fact still remains that there will be days when either the student or the teacher won't be able to cope with the situation.

These days should never occur, but they do. The problem that remains is to find out how a teacher may gracefully handle such a situation. In using this technique, there are some important guidelines to consider:

1. Systematic exclusion should not be used as a blanket device to maintain class order.

2. Systematic exclusion is not employed on the spur of the moment.

3. Contact with the home has to be made prior to using systematic exclusion.

4. Systematic exclusion must be part of a total school plan for handling a particular child.

If these guidelines are followed, and if a reasonable and carefully designed plan is laid out for the child, then systematic exclusion should serve as a healthy substitute for many of the practices currently being used.

Comments: *Isolation and systematic exclusion should be used to protect the students and the teacher. They should* *not be used as punishment with the understanding that a student is being sentenced to spend so much time in the isolation booth. They should be used to avoid a punitive confrontation between the child and the teacher.*

The timeout area should be discussed with the class prior to its use. Students should know what is expected when they are directed to go to a timeout area, they should know how they are supposed to react to someone in the timeout area, and they should know what the general follow-up procedure is for someone who has been in the timeout area. The use of systematic exclusion requires a meeting between the teacher, the child, the child's parents, and other involved personnel. All details and expectations have to be worked out prior to the use of systematic exclusion. In both cases, this is a stopgap measure and should not be viewed as a punishment.

SUSPENSIONS AND CORPORAL PUNISHMENT

Suspensions

Suspensions, whether they take place in school or out of school, should be reserved for extreme cases. They should represent a last-ditch effort.

Suspensions should be limited to one to three days. Generally speaking, you should always hold a parent conference before suspending a child. Following a successful conference, it is a good technique to reduce the suspension time.

In-school suspensions are designed to be used in place of detentions or out-of-school suspensions. Usually, a room will be designated for use by students assigned to in-school suspension, an aide will be assigned supervision responsibilities for this room, and work should be highly structured and closely monitored. In-school suspensions are usually delayed for 24 hours to allow the teacher to provide work for the student to complete during the suspension and to allow for parent contact. Before the child returns to his class, a conference should be held with the student, the teacher, and the principal. A follow-up conference should also be held with the student's parents.

Corporal Punishment

Although it is legal in some states, the use of corporal punishment is very questionable. When you hit a child, you're modeling aggressive behavior. This is the kind of physical aggression that most teachers want students to avoid. Striking a child is seldom, if ever, a natural consequence of misbehavior. If the student is so incorrigible that you must use physical punishment to get your message across, it would be better to remove the child from the class or the school than to hit him.

If you are forced into a situation where corporal punishment is the assigned punishment for a given offense, be sure to follow the general guidelines established by courts:

1. An adult witness should be present.
2. Do not administer punishment if you are excessively angry or emotional.
3. The punishment should be reasonable, given the nature of the offense, the age of the child, and the physical condition of the child.
4. The child should have been forewarned that the punishment would be the consequence of the given misbehavior.

PRINCIPLE: **Restraint and corporal punishment are not the same.**

Restraint will be necessary when someone's well-being is threatened. Restraint should not be viewed as punishment. A teacher should take whatever action is reasonable and necessary in stopping a child from hurting himself or someone else.

Comments: Suspensions and corporal punishment are harsh measures. Because of the potential for negative side effects, these measures are usually self-defeating.

In-school suspensions have proven to be a better alternative in many cases to detentions and out-of-school suspensions; however, they should be used infrequently and only when the well-being of others is at stake.

Most classroom problems are the result of poor judgment and they should not be solved with punitive measures. When a student repeatedly causes a problem, openly defying school policy, stronger measures may be needed. Punishment may help subdue the problem, but chances are that the problem will be displaced and not solved.

Communication should be the main tool for handling the socially remedial child. Parents, staff, and classmates all need help. You have a responsibility to communicate this need and to help others understand the implications of their responsibilities.

With extreme cases, suspension may be needed. Corporal punishment should rarely, if ever, be used. In evaluating your use of punishment, consider the criteria listed in Figure 11-2.

Criteria for Evaluating Disciplinary Measures

Use the following criteria for evaluating the appropriateness of your management techniques:

1. Has the alternative significantly reduced the incidence of undesirable behavior over a period of time?

2. Do the students involved get to continue their education in a meaningful way while involved in the disciplinary process?

3. Does the alternative respect the students' human and due process rights?

4. Is the effect of the alternative to help the student develop self-discipline? Does it build dependence or independence?

5. Does the alternative represent an honest effort to identify and treat the discipline problem, whether it lies with the student, the school personnel, the community, the curriculum, or other factors?

6. Does the alternative recognize the importance of the parents' role? Does it include elements of outreach, respect, and involvement of parents in an effort to provide support to the student involved in the disciplinary process?

Source: "Editorial," by M. Hayes Mizell, **Creative Discipline,** Volume 1, Number 1, August 1977,

Figure 11-2

published by the Southeastern Public Education Program, American Friends Service Committee, 401 Columbia Building, Columbia, South Carolina, 29201.

Figure 11-2 (cont'd)

SUMMARY

In considering punishment and its appropriate use, it is helpful to distinguish between (1) talking or conferring with a student, (2) punishments which follow as a natural consequence, and (3) punishments which are arbitrarily selected. Of the three, a private conference held during class, at recess, or after school has the greatest potential for solving a problem and the least potential for negative side effects. The use of punishments which follow as natural consequences are preferable to arbitrarily selected punishments used as negative contingencies.

In today's schools, there is no excuse for the use of some of the "traditional" punishments:

- Copying a dictionary page.
- Writing 100 sentences: "I will not talk in class."
- Detention—merely "serving time."
- Standing on tiptoes with nose in a circle on the blackboard.
- Standing in the corner or out in the hall.
- Three swats with a paddle.

This chapter developed the following guidelines for using punishment:

- Avoid harsh punishment.
- Always explain why a punishment is being used.
- Don't use delayed or long-term punishment.
- Don't use mass punishment unless the group is either condoning or supporting the misbehavior.
- Don't use exclusion from learning experiences as a punishment.
- Don't punish the child who has a poor self-concept.

Suggestions and guidelines were given for the use of isolation, systematic exclusion, in-school suspensions, and corporal punishment. In the last section, a list of criteria was presented to use in evaluating your own disciplinary measures.

Punishment is a legitimate teaching device; however, it should only be used when someone's well-being is at stake. Punishment does not solve problems; it merely deals with symptoms. Punishment encourages an adversary relationship and has the potential for a variety of negative side effects. Punishment is a legitimate teaching device, but it should be used sparingly and careful consideration should be given to the guidelines presented here.

12

Using Praise and
Positive Reinforcement Effectively

1. Basic Principles to Follow in Using Praise and Positive Reinforcement

   • Praise and positive reinforcement are not necessarily the same.

   • Specific praise is more effective than general praise.

   • Praise the act and not the child.

   • Stress the reason why something is good; avoid stressing your approval.

   • Do not use comparative praise.

   • Give individual praise privately.

   • Avoid praising students who seek approval.

   • If the child is once rewarded with praise, then the later withholding or lack of praise can signify failure.

   • There is an opportunity cost every time you praise a child.

   • Don't use praise unless it is deserved.

   • Praise from an outsider is more effective than praise from the teacher.

   • Praise is best suited for introductory lessons when new material has to be clarified.

2. Ways to Encourage Without Using Praise

   • You can encourage by referring to past accomplishments.

   • You can encourage by indicating possible next steps to take.

   • You can encourage by discussing difficult aspects of tasks that were accomplished.

3. How to Let Students Know They're Learning

4. Ethics of Praise

BASIC PRINCIPLES TO FOLLOW IN USING
PRAISE AND POSITIVE REINFORCEMENT

Praise and positive reinforcement are not necessarily the same. This is an important distinction to make. Positive reinforcement is anything that encourages someone to do something again. If you tell me you like my new suit, I'll probably wear it again; if I notice that sales go up when I wear that suit, I'll probably select it for important deals; and, if I experience an emotional lift from wearing a particular suit, I'll wear it on days when I need an extra kick.

In the first example, praise is a social reward. In the second, commissions resulting from improved sales act as a concrete reward. In the third example, my good feeling is simply an intrinsic reward.

On the other side of the ledger, praise can act as a negative reinforcer. If Flashy Freddie says he likes my coat, I may never wear it again. If I were in seventh grade and the teacher complimented me in front of my peers for helping her after class, that would be the last time I stayed and pushed chairs around. If you tell me my forehand is good, but I overhear you tell Dave that he has a powerful stroke, I may get discouraged. My stroke is not as strong as Dave's. Comparative praise, praise given inappropriately, and praise from someone you don't admire can have a negative effect and discourage your efforts or make you more reluctant to try again. Many things can positively reinforce your behavior. But praise and positive reinforcement are not necessarily the same.

PRINCIPLE: **Praise and positive reinforcement are not necessarily the same.**

Just as there is no simple solution for good classroom management, there is no simple recipe to follow in using praise and positive reinforcement. The effect of praise varies according to the child, the grade level, the time of year, and the nature of the praise. In light of these differential effects, the following principles help to establish parameters and provide guidelines for the use of praise.

PRINCIPLE: **Specific praise is more effective than general praise.**

Comments like "Good paper," "Great work," and "Excellent," lack clarity. They communicate that the teacher is pleased with the work but they don't specifically point out and reinforce the desired behavior. *Try to avoid using the word "good" in isolation. Discipline yourself to pinpoint the specific behavior you want to reinforce.*

- "Your neat margins make the paper easier to read."
- "Excellent descriptive adjectives; I can really picture that old jalopy."
- "Good, I could easily hear the sound effects in the back of the room."

PRINCIPLE: **Praise the act and not the child.**

The following comments praise the child and not the task; therefore, they are undesirable:

- "You're really great! What an excellent story."
- "Wow! Alice, you're quite an artist."
- "I'm really pleased with you. You're really trying."
- "Good, Jim, you certainly have improved."

These comments focus on the child. They give the impression that one's "goodness" or "badness" are determined by how one pleases others. This builds dependence on others for feelings of worthiness. The whole process of teaching should rest on the assumption that we're trying to build *independence*. Focus on the child's behavior. Don't suggest that one's worth depends on judgmental evaluation.

PRINCIPLE: **Stress the reason why something is good; avoid stressing your approval.**

The following comments focus on the teacher's approval and should be avoided:

- "Heather, I like the way you cleaned your desk."
- "Jim, I'm really pleased you have made so much progress."
- "Good work, Jerry. I'll be a happy man if everyone does this well."

Placing the stress on pleasing the teacher works as a positive reinforcer at the primary level but it thwarts maturity (see Chapter 9) and leads to problems at the intermediate level. Pleasing the teacher doesn't work as effectively in the intermediate grades because peer approval begins to displace much of the teacher's influence.

Stressing teacher approval also builds dependence and encourages students to become "other directed." The emphasis should be on the task and the reasons why the behavior is desired, not on the fact that it pleases the teacher. These statements illustrate "good practice":

- "Good, I see that most of you are ready to start."
- "Jim, your studying is paying off. Look at the progress you have made."
- "Good work, Jerry. The floor is really clean; that saves me and the janitor a lot of time."

PRINCIPLE: **Do not use comparative praise.**

Praise should refer to individual progress and should not compare the relative standings of different students. Comparative judgments can give students the idea that they're no good unless they're the best, or at least better than most.

Watch the subtle use of comparative praise. You tell Jim that his answer was good, but you tell Sol that his answer was great. Students hear the difference. How does Jim feel? Was his answer really good?

PRINCIPLE: **Give individual praise privately.**

When you publicly praise an individual, you should focus on something unique, something easily recognized by the other children as being special; otherwise, the students may react negatively. They may feel they did a good job, too, but weren't recognized. Publicly praising individual students can lead to an unwholesome competitiveness as students vie for the teacher's approval. It can also lead to taunts of "teacher's pet." In the intermediate grades, individual public praise can easily weaken group unity. Concentrate on the group:

- "You're making progress. Over half of you have already reached your goal."
- "The fact that most of you remembered to take out your math book saves time. I think we'll be able to work with the In-and-Out Machine at the end of the period."

PRINCIPLE: **Avoid praising students who seek approval.**

Teachers who respond with praise to students who seek approval are less successful in producing student achievement than teachers who react in other ways. Praise usually brings closure. If you probe, you open the door for more learning. Ask a student what he thinks about his work, ask him whether he feels it is right, or ask him what part he likes best. When you do this, you're changing the focus from gaining teacher approval to analyzing the task. In the long run, this will help the student gain independence and self-confidence.

PRINCIPLE: **If the child is once rewarded with praise, then the later withholding or lack of praise can signify failure.**

If one becomes other directed, measuring the worth of one's work on the amount and type of praise received, then one is in for some real highs and lows. Other people are not going to be consistent, with the ebb and flow of their lives, and they cannot consistently feed another person's needs.

The use of praise is a risky business. Teachers who rely heavily on praise to shape student behavior may be doing a disfavor to their students in the long run.

PRINCIPLE: **There is an "opportunity cost" every time you praise a child.**

The few seconds taken to praise a child could be used in a variety of other ways. For example, the teacher could compare one child's idea with another's.

- "How does your idea differ from Phil's?"
- "What does your idea have in common with the others?"

As indicated before, praise brings closure. Analyzing similarities and differences is just one move a teacher can make to stimulate further discussion.

It is interesting to note that research does not show a consistent and significant relationship between praise and student achievement, or between praise and student participation in classroom discussions. However, consistent relationships between probing and student achievement, and between probing and student participation, have been reported.

PRINCIPLE: **Don't use praise unless it is deserved.**

Another problem sometimes overlooked is that your opinion and the student's standards may differ. If you praise work that your student has done that does not meet his own standards, he may lose some respect for your opinion. Or, if your praise comes so easily, he may think that you don't have very high expectations for him and his work. Maybe he's not very capable after all. Praise may sound like mockery or scorn if it is not deserved.

PRINCIPLE: **Praise from an outsider is more effective than praise from the teacher.**

Provide opportunities for your students to receive praise from outsiders. When your class is doing an excellent job, invite the cook, the janitor, the principal, and others to come in and see the good work.

Direct your praise to outsiders. Tell last year's teacher, send a note home to parents, tell your aide or yard duty assistant. These good words will get back to the student and, when they do, they'll carry much more punch.

PRINCIPLE: **Praise is best suited for introductory lessons when new material has to be clarified.**

As a teacher response, specific praise clearly identifies correct examples, interpretations, etc. A judgmental strategy should be used when you're presenting new information to help students identify examples and non-examples; however, when you try to personalize information and help students clarify how a concept relates to their personal lives, you want to use an accepting strategy, you want to encourage discussion among the students, and you want to avoid premature closure. In general, teachers are very capable when it comes to presenting information for students. Too little time is devoted to clarifying information in terms of the students' experiential background, their values, and their current activities. Some of the activities included in this book (see Items 67, 68, 69, 70, and 71) are effective strategies for personalizing concepts. When employing these strategies, teachers should avoid the use of praise and should use nonjudgmental responses (probing, silence, accepting phrases, comparative statements, encouragement, empathy).

> *Comments: Praise should be used. It should be task related, it should be specific, and it should be used when closure is desired. Individual praise should usually be given privately. Public praise should focus on the group's behavior and accomplishments, not the teacher's approval.*
>
> *There is an opportunity cost to using praise. The same amount of time could be used to redirect a question, to compare, or to probe for cause and effect relationships. Praise generally brings closure; therefore, if you want to wrap up a discussion or move on to another point, you can use praise. However, be careful in using praise. Don't unconsciously encourage students to become other directed. You should also avoid comparative judgments which weaken group unity.*

WAYS TO ENCOURAGE WITHOUT USING PRAISE

Praise is judgmental. When you give praise, you state your opinion of a particular behavior or accomplishment. It is usually a summary, passing final judgment; thus, praise brings closure.

- "Jim, that's a good idea."
- "That's an excellent piece of work. Look at all the details."
- "Beverly, you did it again. Another 100 percent. You have really been making progress."

Encouragement gives support and direction. It focuses on the task at hand:

- "Peter, that's an idea that would certainly work. Where would you start?"
- "The project is complicated, so you're going to really have to take it a step at a time."
- "Look at the scores; see the progress you have made?"

Encouragement focuses on the work to be done. Encouragement shows empathy. You understand the problem. *Encouragement builds a closer relationship.* On the other hand, praise is judgmental and connotes a superior/subordinate relationship. *Praise increases social distance.*

Encouragement builds independence. It identifies aspects of the situation, steps involved in meeting the challenge, or past accomplishments which suggest what can be achieved. Encouragement shows understanding and lends support, but it places the responsibility squarely on the shoulders of the person involved. *It builds independence.*

PRINCIPLE: **You can encourage by referring to past accomplishments.**

Reference to past growth helps give perspective. I keep a diary and have done so for the past ten years. When I feel discouraged, reading notations from prior years provides the needed tonic. I can remember how I struggled with things that are second nature now. The needed perspective gives hope and stimulates a renewed effort. Storing samples of student work, taking review tests over earlier work, and keeping logs can provide the same beneficial effects for students.

Consider the value of keeping a cumulative folder of student work (creative writing, artwork, spelling tests, etc.). Have a review day once or twice a month, during which folders are distributed and students can enjoy their past work and add several specimens of which they are particularly proud. The children will enjoy looking back at their past and the folders may prove useful for parent conferences.

Learning takes place along a continuum. You can reinforce a student by calling attention to the progress that has been made:

- "I can remember when you didn't know how to make a capital G."
- "On your first project, you weren't able to countersink the nails. Remember?"
- "You were having trouble telling time at the beginning of the year. Do you remember?"

Rather than praise the new accomplishment, refer to prior problems or to an earlier stage. This emphasizes the growth aspect and allows the student to make his own judgment about "goodness."

PRINCIPLE: **You can encourage by indicating possible next steps to take.**

Positive reinforcement is intended to promote the recurrence of a desired behavior, to encourage continued effort, and to build a positive self-image. If a person has completed part of a project, encouragement could be used to direct the person's attention toward the next step. This demonstrates high expectations, it suggests a "you can do it" attitude, and it leads directly to more accomplishment.

As I mentioned earlier, one of the problems with praise is that you run the risk that the student will feel that the praise was not deserved. This stirs up feelings that say, "Maybe I'm expecting too much, maybe I'm not as good as I thought." In this case, praise may communicate that the teacher doesn't hold very high expectations for the student. Or, if he doesn't feel that the praise was deserved, he may begin to lose faith in your judgment. He may begin to lose respect for you as a teacher. Encouragement—noting past accomplishments or next steps—does not entail this risk.

PRINCIPLE: **You can encourage by discussing difficult aspects of tasks that were accomplished.**

In reacting to a task that a student has completed, you can point out the difficult aspects you see in the task. Students will usually comment on whether they had the same reactions. Pointing out the difficult aspects as you see them leads to further discussion, whereas with praise, students usually just accept the praise or are embarrassed and try to generate a few disclaimers.

- "That's a long list. I would find it difficult to get more than seven or eight items. Did it come easily or did you have to do some real scratching?"

- "The directions in this part appear long and complex. Did you find them hard to follow?"

- "Students say this stage can be boring. Did you have a hard time sticking with the task?"

- "I would find such detail very tedious. Did you?"

When you state a fact or your impression, the discussion remains open and the students can draw their own conclusions. When you use praise, you bring about closure and the students may question your judgment.

HOW TO LET STUDENTS KNOW THEY'RE LEARNING

Nothing succeeds like success. This old saying may be trite, but it's true. You need to give young children visual evidence of the fact that they're learning. They need to see the progress being made. You need to show that today's lesson builds on what they did before and leads on to another step.

If you want good classroom management, students need to see a reason to cooperate. One of the best is knowledge of learning. School is helping them, they are becoming more independent, more resourceful, more capable. Alternatives are opening up for them because they are developing skills.

ITEM 156. A Collage of Learning

Young students can build a collage showing what they have learned (see Figure 12-1). They can start with a house, for they all need a starting point. As each skill is learned, they can add a part to their picture. It is a good idea to have the class generate a long list of possible items to add to the picture (a rabbit, an airplane, a fence, a cloud). This idea provides a visual record of student growth and has

Figure 12-1

an extra in terms of P.R. The collages can be used during conferences.

Edith Jacobson
Northwood, Iowa

ITEM 157. Citizen Sam

You can use Citizen Sam to record good behavior (see Figure 12-2). By folding his legs up underneath him, you can add a pleat each day and make him grow to the ceiling. If the children decide that one of their classmates has been a very special citizen, the legs are lengthened and that child's name is printed on the pleat. The following day, this child is the leader because he was Citizen Sam.

It is important to avoid selecting a child for behavior that wasn't really special. There could be negative spin-offs if others felt they should have been selected too.

Mrs. Agnes Annan
Coin, Iowa

Figure 12-2

ITEM 158. I Have Mastered This Skill

Figures 12-3 and 12-4 show two ways to recognize student accomplishments.

Mrs. Pauline Ruebel
Barnum, Iowa

ITEM 159. Pat on the Back

When your students have worked extra hard on an assignment or have been particularly helpful, one saying is all that's needed to

I know my telephone number. Children add their names and telephone numbers to these sheets.

Figure 12-3

Hang two or three shoes across the top of your board. When children can tie their shoes, they put up paper shoes with their names on them.

Figure 12-4

bring a smile to their faces: "Let's give ourselves a pat on the back for ...." The children will pat their own backs, pat their friends' backs or the teacher will pat their backs. This results in a very proud classroom.

Karen Gundersen
Deerfield, Illinois

ITEM 160. Qwik Quiz

Give short daily quizzes. Start the period with a 3- to 5-minute written "Qwik Quiz." This encourages students to read their daily assignments, see what progress they're making, come to class on time, and get involved in the subject at hand. The quizzes also provide directions in terms of what should be learned and what areas need re-teaching.

Paul Durham
Honolulu, Hawaii

ETHICS OF PRAISE

As teachers, we are professional manipulators. We are paid change agents, paid to stimulate student growth, to help students develop proficiency in the basic skills, to encourage students to use more acceptable social behaviors, to stimulate creative problem solving, to help them become better independent decision makers, and to nurture in them sensitivity toward others. We are paid to change behaviors.

The use of praise is one of our tools. It should be used consciously. We must remember the primary educational goal of building independence.

Praise, when inappropriately used, can build dependence. If we use praise to satisfy our needs for class control, basic questions can be raised. Are we encouraging the students to become other directed? Are we building dependence? As teachers, we want our students to progress away from the need for concrete and social reinforcers and toward reliance on intrinsic reinforcement. Figure 12-5 shows the desired continuum.

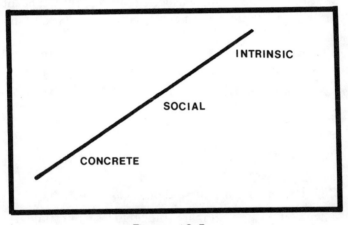

Figure 12-5

If you give students who are already operating at the intrinsic level a heavy dose of social and concrete reinforcement, you run the risk of making them dependent on your reinforcement. The problem will surface when your rewards stop, at which time the student has lost the reason for doing the task. The intrinsic rewards were displaced by the social and concrete ones. The net effect of your behavior is a loss of student interest in the activity. If students are already operating on the intrinsic level, and if they enjoy reading for reading's sake, the use of praise or concrete reinforcers to sustain or increase this interest would be a mistake:

- "Jim, you're doing such a good job reading, if you can read 20 more books by December 1, you can order two free books from our book club."

- "Rayleen, I'm really pleased by the progress you're making. You are really some reader."

You should emphasize the merits of the student's reading. Reinforce their reading by highlighting the intrinsic benefits and use probes and other alternatives to praise:

- "Jim, which books have you enjoyed the most? What made them good reading?"
- "Rayleen, look at the progress you're making. Have you picked up any new ideas on sailing or navigating a small boat?"

SUMMARY

This chapter has stated some of the alternatives to praise and reviewed some of the negative aspects of using praise. The intended message is not that praise is inherently bad, but that praise should be used appropriately.

Alternative strategies can be more effective in developing positive self-concepts and in promoting certain behaviors.

Alternatives to Praise

Silence

Probing

Encouragement

Accepting responses

Comparison and use of student ideas

When you use and compare student ideas, your students realize that they have something to contribute, they become the judges of their own "goodness." This builds independence rather than dependence.

Inappropriately used praise can destroy class unity. It encourages an unhealthy competitiveness as students vie for teacher approval. Praise can breed contempt for the teacher's judgment if the students feel that the teacher's praise was undeserved. In some cases, praise can bring premature closure, aborting the chance for students to personalize the material presented. *Praise should be used, but it should be used consciously in light of alternative responses.*

It is better to accentuate the positive, praise students for their good behavior instead of focusing on undesirable behavior. It is even better to use more sophisticated types of positive reinforcement. You can encourage and positively reinforce by helping students see the progress they have made, by probing and by using student ideas.

13

Successful Ways to Use

Contingency Management Systems

1. Guidelines to Follow in Developing Contingency Management Systems
   - Don't use a system that requires class-wide surveillance.
   - Don't use extrinsic rewards with students who are already achieving success in the area.
   - Examine other alternatives before using a contingency management system.
   - Contingency management systems work effectively with some children.
   - Select concrete reinforcers which are naturally associated with the behavior.
   - Use concrete reinforcers to show a child that he is capable of performing a task.
   - The novelty of a contingency management system has payoff in terms of classroom management.
   - Symbolic rewards are effective at the primary level.
2. Build Class Unity by Using Group Contingencies
3. Examples of Contingency Management Systems

GUIDELINES TO FOLLOW IN DEVELOPING CONTINGENCY MANAGEMENT SYSTEMS

Contingency management, like many educational terms, is a concept clouded by different interpretations and ambiguities. There are believers who strongly support the use of contingency management and those who convincingly argue against it. The arena is clouded by conflicting research, theories, and rhetoric.

Much of the conflict can be attributed to inconsistencies in definitions, teaching techniques, and the children and conditions involved. If you examine the basic components of the theory, there seems to be general agreement on the following:

1. *Accentuate the positive.* Reinforce the student when he is on-task and ignore him when he exhibits undesirable behavior. This is probably most effectively done *publicly* with preschool and primary aged children. With intermediate children, praise should be given *privately* or directed publicly to the whole group (see Chapter 12).

2. *Use positive reinforcement rather than punishment.* Much of the success of contingency management comes from the fact that teachers are forced to look for desired behavior and think in terms of rewards, not punishment. There is little disagreement with the idea that if you accentuate the positive and ignore the negative, you're going to be more successful.

The disagreement surrounding contingency management centers on how you accentuate the positive.

3. *Positive reinforcement should immediately follow the desired behavior.* Again, there is little disagreement with this principle of motivation theory.

4. *When you reinforce a child, state specifically why he is being reinforced.* If a child is receiving a token for some good behavior, the token should be accompanied by specific praise, clearly stating what was desirable about the behavior. Again, there is little disagreement

here. Clarity, whether it is associated with giving directions or giving praise, is an important correlate of effectiveness.

5. *Reward approximations toward the goal.* Setting reasonable expectations, breaking the task down, and providing the needed crutches to help a student achieve success are universally accepted components of good teaching. Using small steps and frequent rewards is particularly important with young children and students of low ability.

Part of the controversy in the field over the use of contingency management comes from the fact that a teacher can break down a task, reward successive approximations, be very specific, and be positive without using a contingency management system. Too often, research compares teachers who lack skill in these areas with teachers receiving training in these areas along with training in contingency management. When you read about contingency management, terms such as concrete reinforcer, behavior modification, contracts, and token economics come to the fore. In this text, the phrase *contingency management system* refers to *any agreement which has been discussed with or explained to a student that specifically establishes that when he does one particular thing, he will be rewarded in one particular manner.* Usually, the rewards are concrete in nature. Typical rewards used by teachers include:

1. More free time (students can pick a game to play, read, work in an interest area, draw, etc.).
2. Playing records (music will be played during a work period).
3. Pick a film to see (students are allowed to look through the AV catalogue and pick their favorite film). TV programs have been used in the same way.
4. Popcorn pop (students are given the chance to prepare and eat a treat).
5. Tokens to use in an auction or in a school store.
6. The privilege to spend time somewhere or with someone:
   - Time in the library.
   - Eat lunch with the teacher.
   - Go out to lunch with the principal.
7. Take a special piece of equipment out at recess:
   - "Nerf" football reserved for use only on special occasions.

- Hoppity Hop.
- Unicycle.
- Paddle ball.
- Special soccer ball, basketball, baseball with a celebrity's signature.
- Special bat or baseball glove.

8. Privilege to keep something on their desks:
   - Add a star to their name tags.
   - Keep a stuffed animal at their desks.
   - Keep a set of special markers or colored pencils.
   - Get a ball of clay to use during free time.
   - A special set of games (the games many parents use to keep children occupied while traveling are good).
   - A special book (cartoon book, book of mazes, sack of funny books).

9. Notes home to parents (these notes may carry a special stamp, blue stars, ribbons, teacher's or principal's written comments).

10. Special classifications:
    - *Rovers* (free to move about the room without having to get permission)
    - *First in line* (for special activities, recess, etc.)

11. The student's picture is taken and given to the student with a note to the parent, or added to a bulletin board in the faculty lounge with a reminder for teachers to congratulate this student.

Contingency management systems work. They have their place; however, caution is recommended in their use.

PRINCIPLE: **Don't use a system that requires class-wide surveillance.**

It is almost impossible for a teacher or aide to monitor a whole class without overlooking behaviors that should be reinforced or making judgmental errors in terms of what is appropriate and inappropriate behavior. Also, the time it takes to run a class-wide system is prohibitive. If you invest this same amount of time in direct tutoring or in planning highly motivational lessons, it could pay greater dividends.

PRINCIPLE: Don't use extrinsic rewards with students who are already achieving success in the area.

As I indicated in Chapter 12, your goal should be intrinsic motivation. You want your students to choose a certain activity or display a certain behavior because they see its value or enjoy it for its own sake. The use of contingency management may change the focus from the activity to the reinforcer. You don't want the reinforcer to undermine existing interest, making a person who was independently choosing an activity become dependent on a reward doled out by others. It should be stressed that the desired behavior should be secondary to the student's decision to exhibit the behavior. You want a child to see why cooperation is desired and freely choose to cooperate. Using the promise of a reward or the threat of punishment to get cooperation may be necessary in some cases, but it is certainly not the desired objective. *Don't use extrinsic rewards with students who are already displaying the desired behavior.*

PRINCIPLE: Examine other alternatives before using a contingency management system.

Contingency management systems place the focus on behavior and not on the causes of behavior. The causes of many undesirable behaviors can be diagnosed and treated. A premature decision to shape behavior with a contingency management system can mask the problem and circumvent treatment, leading to more serious consequences in the long run.

PRINCIPLE: Contingency management works effectively with some children.

Children who make decisions on a basic pleasure/pain level may respond very favorably to a contingency management system. Many young children and some intermediate youngsters will respond best to concrete reinforcers. These rewards motivate, but it should be remembered that they build dependency. A heavy dose of concrete rewards would be detrimental for most students because concrete reinforcers dissipate one's energy.

PRINCIPLE: **Select concrete reinforcers which are naturally associated with the behavior.**

As with punishment (see Chapter 11), you want the reinforcer to naturally follow from the activity. For example:

1. If a class uses its time wisely, the teacher might respond by having them play a favorite activity during the last five minutes of the class period. Earlier, the class may have listed seven activities they like to play. One of these could be drawn from the hat, and those students who want to participate could quickly do so. The class was efficient, so the reward of free time follows naturally.

2. If a student gets good grades on his report card, he might be allowed to call his grandmother and tell her the good news. This seems to follow much more naturally than getting paid for the good grades.

3. If a child gets his homework completed for class, he might be given more freedom during work periods. He might be able to get out of his seat without permission, to use the microscope for five minutes during the work period, etc. In other words, he finished his task, so his reward is free choice of an array of fun activities.

In the above examples, the reward follows naturally. Here, the use of concrete reinforcers serves as informational feedback. The reward is related to the activity and is either a type of intrinsic motivation or leads to intrinsic motivation.

PRINCIPLE: **Use concrete reinforcers to show a child that he is capable of performing a task.**

Some children need an "extra" motivator to overcome inertia and the fear of failure. A prize or chance to win a prize can provide the extra push that may be needed. In these cases, the use of the reinforcer should be short-lived.

I might offer my reluctant ten-year-old one free game on a pinball machine for every attempt he makes at trying to water ski. The reward is offered to give him the extra push to try. This is a one-time reward used to help him learn that he is capable, that he *can* do it.

PRINCIPLE: **The novelty of a contingency management system has payoff in terms of classroom management.**

A token economy is novel and will build student interest for a short period of time. It could be used as a change of pace rather than a stopgap measure used to fight a crisis situation.

As I indicated earlier, the classroom is an organized group and has certain needs as such. Some techniques can be legitimized because they meet the group's needs rather than individual needs.

Used for the sake of variety or as an antidote for "cabin fever," some class-wide contingency management systems have their places. In these cases, the dosage should be small and should deal with low level skills and/or isolated information.

PRINCIPLE: **Symbolic rewards are effective at the primary level.**

Brophy and Evertson (1976) found symbolic rewards (particularly gold stars and smiling faces placed on papers to be taken home and shown to parents, or placed on charts in the room) to be positively associated with learning gains at the primary level.

Comments: Contingency management systems have their place. They work best on an individual basis with students who do not respond favorably to social or intrinsic rewards. In these cases, it is important to remember that you're merely shaping behavior; you're doing little to change the factors causing or influencing the undesirable behavior. When a contingency management system is established, it is best to select a reinforcer which has a logical relationship to the desired behavior. Contingency management systems also have their place as a novel change of pace, making the doldrums of school more palatable.

BUILD CLASS UNITY BY USING
GROUP CONTINGENCIES

Many teachers offer rewards to the best row, the first table finished, the quietest group, and those who get 100 percent or miss less than five. Most of these rewards force a win/lose situation which can spawn unhealthy competitiveness in the class. Students may pick on a certain student because they feel he has caused them to lose (not being first means losing). Or, students may feel that the teacher is not being fair—Susie's row is always first.

Rather than offer rewards to the best, the fastest, and the cleanest, consider other options. Johnson and Johnson (1975) have researched the use of three different types of group contingencies:

1. *Average performance group contingency.* The members of the group are rewarded on the basis of the average performance of all the group members. "If the average score is 80 percent or higher, you get to..."

2. *High performance group contingency.* The scores of the highest one-quarter of the group are used as a basis for determining rewards. "If the average of the top five students is at least 95 percent, we will..."

3. *Low performance group contingency.* The scores of the lowest one-quarter of the group are used as a basis for determining rewards. "If the average of the lowest five scores is at least above 70 percent, we will..."

Johnson and Johnson (1975) have reported that the low performance group is the most effective in terms of raising achievement test scores and in terms of developing a helping, healthy attitude among students. The capable students can tutor and root for the less able. This cooperative spirit will build class unity and has been shown not to be detrimental in any way to the top students. Average class scores are the highest when the reward is tied to the performance of the lowest quarter of the class.

You might experiment with some of the following arrangements. (*Note:* In each case, enough leeway is provided to accommodate a few problems, errors in judgment, or poor performances.)

1. "If I only have to remind five students to be quiet during this morning, the whole class will get five minutes added to their afternoon recess."

2. If all but three pass the desk check, then you'll be allowed to take the book sacks to your desks for reading during free time."

3. "If the lowest five scores in our group average over 75 percent, then we'll devote Friday's math period to your choice of math games."

4. If all but two groups successfully answer the problems, then we'll let you have the last 10 minutes of the period to start on your homework."

In each of the cases above, an attempt has been made to make the reward a natural contingency of the behavior. Students should be encouraged to help each other keep the noise down, to check each other's desks and suggest ways to better organize them, to drill each other, and so on. You still run the risk of having one or two students pinpointed as the goats for having done poorly or spoiling it for the rest. As the teacher, you need to stress the group's responsibility. If you work with averages and leave a good margin of error, you will reduce the chance of pinpointing or focusing the class's misery on one student.

> *Comments: If you focus on the best row, the top five, or those who get 100 percent, you're not helping those who see themselves as not having a chance. You're encouraging an elitist attitude and discouraging a helping, caring concern for each other. The top students will continue to perform at a high level; they're self-motivated in most cases. Working together and supporting each other will build class unity which will make peer pressure more effective in managing the class. When you base the contingency on the performance of the bottom quarter or lowest ten scores, your low ability students will benefit from the attention, make better progress, and improve their self-images. This will result in fewer conflicts and a reduction in the use of misbehavior as a device for getting attention. It is a win/win situation.*

EXAMPLES OF CONTINGENCY MANAGEMENT SYSTEMS

The following systems have been used in the classroom and contributors report that they are effective in shaping student behavior. They should be examined and their use weighed in terms of the principles presented. Keep in mind that the strategies may be appropriate for some students and not for others. The strategies may also work as a good change of pace and not merely as a way of coping with undesirable behavior.

ITEM 161. Super Kids

Work with your students to identify specific goals. A ditto can be used so that the goals can be prepared in contract form. The goals should be individually tailored, challenging but still reasonable expectations.

Enlarge a picture of Superman and add the caption: "These Super Kids accomplished their goals."

When the students accomplish their goals, they sign their names on the bulletin board and also receive paper emblems like Superman's to wear on their shirts (see Figure 13-1).

Mrs. Karen Asa
Algona, Iowa

Figure 13-1

ITEM 162. Beat Your Mark

After the students have taken at least six spelling tests, figure the average number missed for each child. These become their marks. A sticker or stamp is awarded each Friday to those students who beat their marks.

A poster is another type of reward. Those students who beat their marks get to draw for a poster.

Christine Benedict
St. Charles, Iowa

ITEM 163. Smarty Cards

Job cards can be used to direct the activity of the early finishers and students with free time (see Figure 13-2). Students have reacted more favorably to the cards when the name was changed from Job Card to Smarty Card.

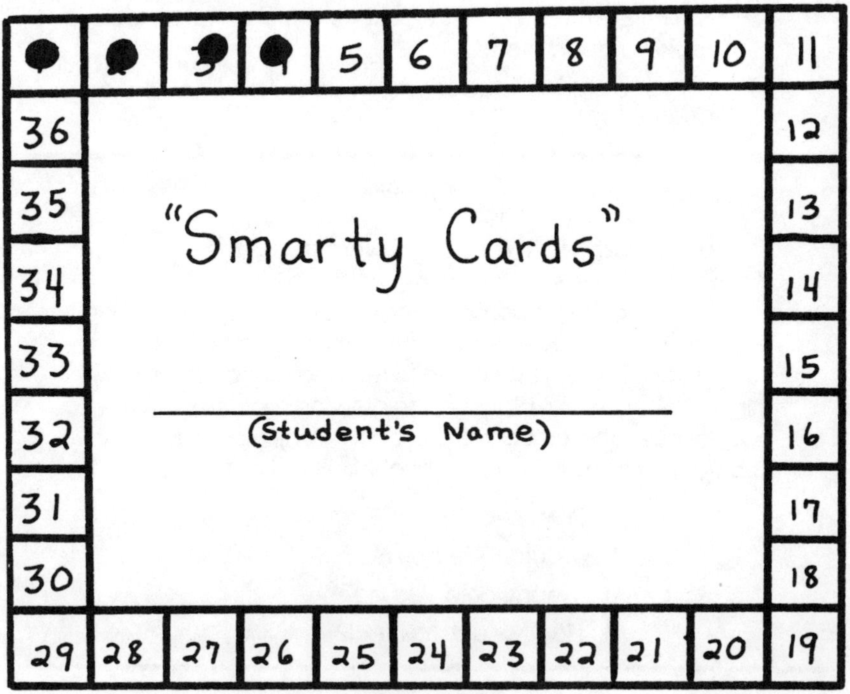

Figure 13-2

A Smarty Card is a 4″ × 6″ filing card on which are listed jobs or tasks designed to develop specific skills. When a child demonstrates mastery of the tasks listed on his card, he then gets to punch a hole in a card for his record.

If a teacher wishes, after a designated number of punches, a child can pick a little prize from a treasure chest and go on with more Smarty Cards.

There can be some easy and some hard skills to master. There is much incentive and it works well.

Some sample cards are shown in Figure 13-3. The list can go on and on to suit the teacher and his or her needs.

Glenna Rhine
New Sharon, Iowa

Smarty Card

Comprehension: Making Judgments and Drawing Conclusions

1. Choose a story character whom you would like to have as a friend. Tell why you believe this character would make a good friend.
2. Name a story character whom you would **not** like to have for a friend. Tell why.

Smarty Card

It was a very dark night. There were stars in the sky . . . like diamonds above. But, the moon hadn't come up yet.

Mike and Tom had gone for a walk in the woods, but now it seemed they were lost. They were getting cold and hungry, too. The boys sat down to rest and found themselves thinking about warm blankets, the glowing campfire, and the good supper the others were probably enjoying. Suddenly, through the trees they saw a bright ball of light.

1. What was it?
2. Would it be harmful?
3. What would you do?
4. How would you feel?

Smarty Card

Comprehension: Figurative Speech

1. Authors have a way of helping us "see" things more clearly. They use figurative speech, such as:

      as clear as a bell

      as happy as a lark

      as sly as a fox

2. Skim several stories for figurative speech. Make a list.

Figure 13-3

ITEM 164. Free Time Pass

This system helps motivate students to complete assigned work. A grid is used daily by the teacher to show completed assignments (see Item 121. The Slate). The last 20 minutes of each day is set aside as an activity period. If a student has turned in all assignments for the day, he gets a free time ticket which he puts in a decorated can (see Figure 13-4). He can then use the 20 minutes of free time for playing games or another free time activity. At the end of each month, the can is opened and the tickets are sorted and counted. The five students with the most tickets are given an award paper showing this accomplishment and a treat.

Figure 13-4

You could use the group award instead of the individual award by stating:

- "If all but three of you have at least five slips, the class gets ..." (This is a low group contingency.)
- "If the total number of tickets is over 300 for the month, the class will ..." (This is a contingency based on the average performance.)

Adapted from an idea submitted by:
Mary Kilburg
Boulder, Colorado

ITEM 165. Neat Table Badge

In the primary grades, each group of students could have a "Neat Table Badge" which they put out at the end of the day (see Figure 13-5). After the children leave, if the table is neat, a star is put on the badge. If the table isn't neat, the badge is picked up. The next day the students can't leave until they have earned their badges back.

Francis Bayles
Oelwein, Iowa

Figure 13-5

ITEM 166. A Bag Full of Peanuts

Post the following poem on a bulletin board:

Read, read, read some more!
Use peanuts to keep your score.
Put them in your bag; you can't eat.
Turn in five for a treat.
Fill your bag to a larger size.
Then you'll get a better prize.

On either side and under the poem, hang small paper sacks with a student's name written on each one. Have a manila folder for each child with his name on it and a can full of white foam peanuts (the kind frequently used for packing in packages).

Each time a child reads a book, he fills out a book report form, adds it to his folder, takes a peanut from the can, and puts it into his paper sack on the bulletin board. When he has five peanuts in the bag, he can cash them in for five real peanuts and a coupon. The coupon is put in the class bag. If, at the end of the month, there are 20 coupons in the class bag, the class is rewarded with a desired activity.

Adapted from an idea submitted by:
Mrs. Ann Stroebele
Oakland, Iowa

ITEM 167. Point Count

As an incentive for a class to think about working quietly, have the class list times when they should be quiet. Give a point value for each of these times.

1. Quiet as we enter the room: 10 points
2. Quiet in the halls, going to music or the library: 10 points
3. Quiet during the reading period: 15 points
4. Quiet during story time: 5 points

Help the class set a goal for the week of how many "Quiet Points" they should be able to earn (see Figure 13-6). During the day at the appropriate time, points can be added to a running total.

Figure 13-6

If the class meets their goal, they can select a group activity: play a game, free time, a bubble gum chew, etc. Each time the class accomplishes their goal, they should set the next goal at least five points higher.

Mrs. Jackie Anderson
Anita, Iowa

ITEM 168. Positive Behavior Charts

When a particular problem develops, have the class identify specific behaviors that are needed to correct the system. For example, if your students are having trouble coming in from recess and settling down to work, the class might devise a chart similar to the one shown in Figure 13-7.

Items	M	T	W	TH	F	Total
1. Take out the books or materials to be studied after recess.						
2. Stop playing immediately when the bell rings (no "Sunday Shots," no kicking the ball or bouncing the ball, etc.).						
3. Walk directly to the line (no drinks, etc.).						
4. Start right to work when you enter the room.						

Figure 13-7

All rules are listed in a positive manner. At the end of the day, time is reserved for the students to evaluate their day and record their points. When a preestablished number of points is reached, a reward is given. It is important that the students make the rules, that they have a copy of them at their desks, and that sufficient time is allowed for evaluation at the end of the day (sometimes they may need to evaluate immediately after each recess). This may be run on an individual, group, or class basis.

Helen E. Armstrong
St. Charles, Iowa

ITEM 169. Earn and Learn

In this activity, children earn special privileges by completing specific tasks.

Present the class with a list of five or six ways to earn "special privileges." Have the students contribute other ideas and also discuss the privileges that could be earned.

As a student earns a privilege, he is given an acknowledgment signed by the teacher (see Figure 13-8). Arrangements should be made at this time to the mutual satisfaction of both the student and the teacher about when the student may use the "privilege."

Earn and Learn Acknowledgment

This shows that _____ has
                        (student's name)

satisfactorily completed _____ and
                            (task)

is entitled to _____ on
                    (special privilege)

_____ ___
(day of the week)

at _____ .
        (time of day)

_____
(teacher's signature)

Figure 13-8

Earn and Learn Special Privileges

1. Play a game on the Magic Square. (Students may bring a game of their own or use a class game. The Magic Square is a washable bathroom rug.)
2. Read a book on the Magic Carpet.
3. Make things from the Odds and Ends Box (see Item 32, Workshop, for related ideas). In this case, the box could contain such items as popsicle sticks, spools, plastic spoons, straws, ice cream dishes, styrofoam meat trays, pieces of jewelry—anything that a creative mind could use.
4. Go to the Media Center to browse or read.

ITEM 170. Personal Note to the Student

Notes such as the one shown in Figure 13-9 can help motivate your students and build positive rapport with parents.

Miss Kline
Iowa City, Iowa

Figure 13-9

ITEM 171. Scheduled Time Check

For a child who has difficulty listening or staying on-task, make a ditto with clocks and a chart to be placed on the child's desk (see Figure 13-10). Use a check, plus, or star to indicate when the child works well. You may want from one to three checking times a day, depending on the child.

Pat Schabinger
Chicago, Illinois

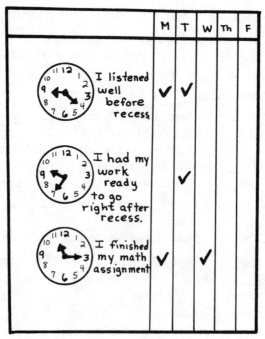

Figure 13-10

ITEM 172. A Point System for Music Teachers

Classes can earn points according to a schedule such as the one displayed in Figure 13-11.

Points	Item
1	Per minute of good cooperative class-work (35 minutes equals 35).
1 (2)	Per student who is working well. Double points when everyone works well the entire class period.
1 to 3	Entering quietly, getting out supplies, and being ready to work.
3	New song well done.
1	Old song reviewed.
1	Warm-up exercises
2	Singing well together.
2	Working well together.
1	Correct answer.
2	Listening quietly.
3	Listening and singing, moving, creating together.
3	Cleaning up quietly and leaving in an orderly manner.
?	Bonus points for extras which add interest and demonstrate skills. This covers a large area—performance, original ideas, assistance to teacher or other students, etc.

Figure 13-11

When a class reaches a set number of points, they are rewarded.

Donna Williams
Cedar Rapids, Iowa

ITEM 173. The Principal Presents a Certificate

Make a set of 3" × 5" flashcards for every student (you can use the old cards from the library card catalog). Each child works at his own pace. He begins with zeroes and adds the ones when he shows he has learned the zeroes. When the child has mastered his number facts he receives a "certificate" presented by the principal in front of the class.

Ruth Noelck
Vail, Iowa

SUMMARY

Most contingency management systems use concrete rewards to shape student behavior. If used appropriately, these systems are effective in shaping student behavior. They are, however, easily abused and certain pitfalls should be avoided.

1. Avoid using systems which require class-wide surveillance of individual students. It is next to impossible to be fair while trying to keep track of all your students. Furthermore, a class-wide system is generally too time consuming.

2. Avoid using concrete reinforcers when the students already respond favorably to social and intrinsic rewards.

3. Remember that contingency management systems shape behavior, not the perceptions causing the behavior.

4. Intrinsic motivation builds independence; concrete reinforcers build dependence.

5. Avoid systems which pit student against student and create a win/lose situation in your class.

6. Avoid systems which are focused on the top performers. These systems can build elitism and can be discouraging and frustrating to the less able.

7. Avoid systems that are negatively oriented, systems that require the teacher to penalize, to take points away. Accentuate the positive; do not call attention to the negative.

Contingency management systems work best with young children and children who basically rely on the pleasure/pain principle for making decisions. Try to capitalize on some of the following:

1. The use of symbolic rewards is positively correlated with student achievement at the primary level.

2. The use of contingency management pays dividends in terms of motivation (novelty). It can be used best on a short-term basis to motivate routine or procedural matters such as room cleanup, meeting deadlines, or turning in assignments.

3. Use reinforcers which follow naturally from the desired behavior because they help foster intrinsic motivation.

4. Concrete reinforcers can be used to give a child that extra push to show him that he is capable of performing a task.

If you're using a contingency management system as your main tool for controlling a class, chances are you're using it inappropriately. It may work, but you are not helping the children to mature. You are solving your needs for a quiet, manageable class at the expense of your students' growth. Some students may need to be working on one system or another all year, but these are socially remedial cases. Most young children will respond very favorably to a contingency management system but, again, you're not modeling a higher level of reasoning and you're therefore not promoting the students' growth. Contingency management systems have their place, but they are easily abused.

CONCLUSION

Classroom management is a complex issue. It's unrealistic and naive to think that most behavior problems are going to be solved with a given technique or strategy. Simple cause and effect relationships do not exist. You're not going to find simple answers to complex problems.

Successful classroom managers want their students to enjoy learning. They want students to be motivated, to readily participate, to be inquisitive, to care, and to grow into rational, independent decision makers. Successful managers strive for intrinsic motivation. They reject aversive motivation, punitive reactions, and win/lose situations. They try to solve problems by engineering, not by reacting.

Successful classroom managers avoid problems, they try to capture rather than coerce, they hold high expectations, they try to dignify students, and they have a large repertoire of activities, techniques, and strategies. They make decisions consciously, not out of habit or default. Their values, rhetoric, and actions are consistent and purposeful.

The ideas presented in this book are practical. They are classroom tested. They work. They provide alternatives which can help you cope with some of the diversity found in classrooms. *The more ideas, techniques, and strategies you have, the more effective you'll be.*

Bibliography

Beyer, Barry K., "Conducting Moral Discussions in the Classroom," *Social Education,* April 1976, pp. 194-202.
This article provides excellent background information dealing with Kohlberg's Levels of Moral Decision Making. A teaching strategy is presented as well as specific techniques and principles.

Borich, Gary D., *The Appraisal of Teaching,* Addison-Wesley Publishing Company, 1977, pp. 71-194.
A scholarly analysis of teacher effectiveness research, techniques for measuring teacher performance, the application of performance appraisal systems, and the use of appraisal techniques and procedures.

Brophy, Jere E., and Evertson, Carolyn M., *Learning from Teaching: A Developmental Perspective,* Allyn and Bacon, Inc., 1976.
An excellent review of teacher effectiveness research. Of particular interest are distinctions made dealing with the relative effectiveness of various teacher techniques on high socio-economic status children as compared with low socio-economic status children.

Brophy, Jere E., and Good, Thomas L., *Teacher-Student Relationships*, Holt, Rinehart and Winston, Inc., 1974.
An analysis of research related to teacher-student interaction patterns, teacher expectations, and other areas related to teacher effectiveness.

Canfield, Jack, and Wells, Harold C., *100 Ways to Enhance Self-Concept in the Classroom: A Handbook for Teachers and Parents,* Prentice-Hall, Inc., 1976.
The title is very descriptive. This is an excellent collection of ideas which can add to any elementary teacher's repertoire of activities, techniques, and strategies.

Chase, Larry, *The Other Side of the Report Card: A How-to-Do-It Program for Affective Education,* Goodyear Publishing Co., Inc., 1975.
This text provides very practical suggestions for starting and guiding class meetings. An excellent book for the practitioner dealing with the affective component of teaching.

Chess, Stella, M.D.; Thomas, Alexander, M.D.; and Birch, Herbert G., M.D., *Your Child Is a Person: A Psychological Approach to Parenthood Without Guilt,* The Viking Press, 1965.
The focus of this text is on the young child from infancy to first grade. It is a good general source of ideas related to parent/child and teacher/child relationships.

Combs, Arthur W.; Avila, Donald L.; and Purkey, William W., *Helping Relationships: Basic Concepts for the Helping Professions,* Allyn and Bacon, Inc., 1971.
This is a must book for anyone who works with people. My ideas on the importance of perceptions were greatly influenced by these authors.

Dewey, John, *Interest and Effort in Education,* Houghton Mifflin Company, 1913.
Dewey eloquently argues for intrinsic motivation. Reading this small text can provide considerable insight into the wisdom and folly of contingency management as a motivational tool.

Dreikurs, Rudolf, *Maintaining Sanity in the Classroom: Illustrated Teaching Techniques,* Harper and Row, 1971.
This text presents a cohesive theory for reacting to and interacting with students. Anyone interested in helping children mature should read this text.

Dreikurs, Rudolf, and Cassel, Pearl, *Discipline Without Tears,* Hawthorn Books, Inc., 1972.
This text presents a cohesive set of practical principles of conflict resolution. Key chapters include: "Encouragement," "Logical Consequences, Not Punishment," "Competition,"

and "The Class Discussion Period." I strongly recommend this book to all principals and teachers.

Duke, Daniel, "Can the Curriculum Contribute to Resolving the Educator's Discipline Dilemma?" *Action in Teacher Education, The Journal of the Association of Teacher Educators,* Vol. 1, No. 2, Fall-Winter 1978, pp. 17-35.
An informative article dealing with using curriculum in both a direct and indirect way to shape student behavior.

Fenton, Edwin, "Moral Education: The Research Findings," *Social Education,* April 1976, pp. 188-193.
This article summarizes Kohlberg's Levels of Moral Reasoning and is an excellent place to start in terms of reading in this area.

Fromm, Erich, *The Art of Loving,* Bantam Books, 1956.
A seminal book providing an analysis of unconditional love and respect for others. A theory is developed stressing the importance of care, responsibility, respect, and knowledge as basic elements of all forms of love.

Glasser, William, M.D., *School Without Failure,* Harper and Row, 1969.
This well-known text is one that should be read and reread by all educators. In particular, the chapters on classroom meetings have been an important resource for me.

Gordon, Thomas, *P.E.T., Parent Effectiveness Training: The Tested New Way to Raise Responsible Children,* Plume Books, 1970.
This well-known source provides specific guidelines for developing and using "I Messages." It is also an excellent source for understanding the importance of a win/win approach.

Holt, John, *What Do I Do Monday?* A Delta Book, 1970.
This book contains many practical suggestions for open-ended independent activities.

Howard, Eugene R., *School Discipline Desk Book,* Parker Publishing Company, Inc., 1978.
A practical book of ideas focusing on high school discipline problems. Sample chapter titles include: "Conducting a Campaign Against Crime and Violence," "Increasing Student Involvement in the School's Activity Program," and

"Achieving More Effective Discipline by Improving Self-Esteem."

Hunter, Madeline, *Reinforcement Theory for Teachers,* TIP Publications, 1967.
This is one in a series of programmed books by this author. All are recommended for basic review of important learning theory.

Hymes, James L., *Behavior and Misbehavior: A Teacher's Guide to Action,* Prentice-Hall, Inc., 1954.
An easy-to-read philosophical text which had an early and very influential effect on my philosophy of teaching.

Johnson, David W., and Johnson, Roger T., *Learning Together and Alone,* Prentice-Hall, Inc., 1975.
All teachers should read this text. It gives an excellent review of research related to the use of competition in the classroom. Reading it will have an impact on your teaching.

Kagan, Jerome, *Understanding Children: Behavior, Motives, and Thought,* Harcourt Brace Jovanovich, Inc., 1971.
A readable source for better understanding of behavior, motives, anger, and perceptions.

Kounin, Jacob S., *Discipline and Group Management in Classrooms,* Holt, Rinehart and Winston, Inc., 1970.
This book reports the findings of a series of studies directed by Kounin. These studies provide helpful definitions and data to better understand effective classroom management. It is must reading for the serious student of teaching.

Madsen, Charles H., Jr., and Madsen, Clifford K., *Teaching/Discipline: Behavior Principles Toward a Positive Approach,* Allyn and Bacon, Inc., 1974.
A good source for understanding the theory and practice behind the use of contingency management systems.

Pennsylvania Department of Education, *Guidelines for School Discipline,* prepared by the Commissioner's Task Force on Student Reponsibility and Discipline, 1976 (order from Pennsylvania Department of Education, Box 911, Harrisburg, PA 19126).

This set of state guidelines deals with such topics as suspensions, expulsions, and consistency and fairness in discipline.

Postman, Neil and Weingartner, Charles, *Teaching As a Subversive Activity,* Delta, 1969.
This book provides insight into the value of being a risk taker and being willing to be vulnerable as a teacher. The value of open-ended teaching is stressed by these authors, as well as the importance of asking why when it comes to deciding what should be taught.

Rosenshine, Barak and Furst, Norma, "Research in Teacher Performance Criteria," *Research in Teacher Education,* edited by B. Othanel Smith for the American Education Research Association, Prentice-Hall, Inc., 1971.
This article reviews process/product teacher effectiveness research. It provides an excellent summary of research.

Rowe, Mary Budd, "Science, Silence, and Sanctions," *Science and Children,* March 1969, pp. 11-13.
This article reviews Rowe's research on the value of using teacher silence as a reaction to student responses.

Shaftel, Fannie R. and Shaftel, George, *Role Playing for Social Values: Decision Making in the Social Studies,* Prentice-Hall, Inc., 1967.
A series of moral dilemmas are provided as well as guidelines for the use of role playing in the classroom.

Stauffer, Russell G., *The Language-Experience Approach to the Teaching of Reading,* Harper and Row, 1970.
This text has been helpful in suggesting open-ended activities to use in designing both independent and teacher directed activities.

Wallen, Carl J. and Wallen, La Donna L., *Effective Classroom Management,* Allyn and Bacon, Inc., 1978.
A comprehensive text which has many good ideas for teachers and administrators. Some of the topics include: "Incentive Techniques," "Parent Communication," "Role Play," "Morale Building," and "Self Concept."

Way, Brian, *Development Through Drama,* Longmans, 1967.
This text presents many practical ideas for using drama as a
tool. An excellent collection of activities, techniques, and
strategies is presented. Any teachers interested in using social
drama or role playing should add this book to their
professional library.

Index

T

U

V

W